WILLIAM
SHAKESPEARE

ON

THE ART OF LOVE

WILLIAM SHAKESPEARE

O N

THE ART OF LOVE

THE ILLUSTRATED EDITION

OF THE MOST BEAUTIFUL LOVE PASSAGES IN SHAKESPEARE'S PLAYS AND POETRY

EDITED BY MICHAEL BEST

DUNCAN BAIRD PUBLISHERS

LONDON

William Shakespeare on The Art of Love

Distributed in the USA and Canada by
Sterling Publishing Co., Inc.
387 Park Avenue South
New York, NY 10016-8810

This edition first published in the USA in 2008 by
Duncan Baird Publishers Ltd
Sixth Floor, Castle House
75–76 Wells Street
London W1T 3QH

Designers: Justin Ford and Luana Gobbo
Picture Research: Julia Brown and Gillian Glasson
Managing Editor: Christopher Westhorp
Managing Designer: Daniel Sturges

Library of Congress Cataloging-in-Publication Data available

ISBN: 978-1-84483-721-2

1 3 5 7 9 10 8 6 4 2

Typeset in Adobe Jenson Pro
Color reproduction by Colourscan, Singapore
Printed in China by Regent

About the editor
Michael Best is the Coordinating Editor of the Internet Shakespeare Editions.
He is Professor Emeritus at the University of Victoria in British Columbia.

Cover and page 2 captions
Cover art: A Tudor Rose, a traditional heraldic emblem of England.
"What's in a name? That which we call a rose
By any other word would smell as sweet. . ."
(from *Romeo and Juliet*—see p.163).
Page 2: William Shakespeare, c.1610, attributed to John Taylor.
(National Portrait Gallery, London.)

For information about custom editions, special sales, premium and corporate
purchases, please contact Sterling Special Sales Department at 800-805-5489
or specialsales@sterlingpub.com.

Note: The following sonnets can be read together – 5/6, 15/16, 27/28, 33/34/35, 40/41/42,
43/44/45, 46/47, 50/51, 57/58 (these two may be reworkings of the same sonnet), 64/65,
67/68, 71/72, 73/74, 82/83, 89/90, 92/93, and 94/95.

Contents

WILLIAM SHAKESPEARE

Introduction

In the film *Shakespeare in Love*, a fictional Queen Elizabeth begins by stating baldly that "playwrights teach nothing about love, they make it pretty, they make it comical, or they make it lust. They cannot make it true", and she bears witness to a wager by Lord Wessex to this effect. After she has (improbably enough) seen the first performance of *Romeo and Juliet* in the public theatre, she changes her mind; to Wessex she says: "There was a wager, I remember . . . as to whether a play can show the very truth and nature of love. I think you lost it today."[1] The movie plays wittily on the likelihood that modern readers will associate Shakespeare and the art of love with his iconic play of tragic young passion and one or two much-anthologized sonnets.

In his own time, Shakespeare was associated more with Ovid, whose works on the art of love (*Ars Amatoria*), on lovers (*Amores*), and on the myths of the loves of the gods (*Metamorphoses*), were avidly read in Latin, and in the popular translation (1567) by Arthur Golding. The first appreciative review of Shakespeare's work was written in 1598 by Francis Meres, a contemporary who had earned a Master of Arts from both Oxford and Cambridge. Meres claimed approvingly that "the sweet witty soul of Ovid lives in mellifluous and honey-tongued Shakespeare". Shakespeare's first publication, the erotic narrative poem *Venus and Adonis*, begins with a quotation from Ovid's *Amores*: in Christopher Marlowe's translation, it reads, "Let base conceited wits admire vile things, / Faire *Phoebus* lead me to the Muses' springs". Shakespeare significantly changes the myth he borrowed from the *Metamorphoses*; in his version even

Convent garden   S. Clement

Somerset h.   Arundel house   Eſſex houſ.   Temple ſtayres   Temple   Blackfreyars

The Globe

Beere bayting

the goddess of Love herself is powerless in her search for love, no matter how persuasive, how artful, she is. The story becomes a kind of creation myth, as Venus prophesies that all following attempts at love thereafter will be fraught with the same anxieties, frustrations, and disappointments (see pp.138–9).

Shakespeare's own portrayal of love is not quite the same as the view he gives Venus. The selection in this volume will demonstrate a wide range of responses, from lyrical to comic to bitter to tragic. It has not been easy to choose representative passages from the immense wealth of Shakespeare's works that focus on love. I have tried to avoid the creation of an anthology of snippets or quotations; too often Shakespeare's words are abstracted from their context and consequently reduced in the richness of their meaning. Some lines are so familiar that they have become clichés, disassociated with their origins; we may, for example, be reminded that one should "neither a borrower nor a lender be", with the writer forgetting that it is silly old Polonius who is boring his children with the truism. Or we may hear splendid advice about the importance of reputation:

> . . . he that filches from me my good name
> Robs me of that which not enriches him
> And makes me poor indeed. (*Othello*, 3.3.170–4.)

But we will not be reminded that these words are spoken by Shakespeare's most consummate villain, Iago, as he works on Othello's insecurities, instilling in him a murderous jealousy. In Shakespeare's works, the character of the speaker gives resonance to the sentiment, proclaiming and questioning it at the same moment. In just the same way, his exploration of love combines triumphant affirmation with deep questioning and anxiety – much of which comes from the context of the passage. For this reason, I have attempted where possible to provide sufficiently complete selections to make clear the interplay of ironies and multiplicities of meaning that are so central to Shakespeare's art.

From the poems, the sonnets are presented in full – dense and challenging as many of them are – as they focus on the interplay of relationships over time. There is a sampling of *Venus and Adonis*, enough to give the flavour of this erotic poem, immensely popular in the period. From the plays I have chosen to include many familiar and justly loved sequences – *Romeo and Juliet* is well represented – together with passages that may be less familiar, from *Love's Labour's Lost*, for example. There are sequences that explore the darker side of love. Richard III woos Lady Anne over the corpse of her father-in-law, Iago manipulates Othello into believing that his wife is unfaithful, and King Leontes explodes in irrational jealousy. There are tragedies, and there are happy endings, however improbable. In all the selections from the plays I provide a sketch of the intervening plot – just enough for those who may not have read the play to grasp the context, with its attendant complexities. Through it all, Shakespeare's language invites us to participate in the feelings of his lovers and to become aware of the multiple layers of irony and paradox that love reveals in human interaction. Because Shakespeare was writing four centuries ago, brief notes are there to assist readers in understanding the way that words have changed and to fill in some of the allusions.

Love in Renaissance society

More has changed than the language, however. The whole social structure, with its attendant expectations of love, friendship, marriage, and family, has changed radically since Shakespeare was writing. Most obviously, the assumption that young lovers today have of freedom of choice was by no means the norm, and the whole impulse of erotic love, so central to Shakespeare's romantic comedies, was regarded with deep suspicion, both for religious and economic reasons. The marriage service Shakespeare would have heard in *The Book of Common Prayer* stresses the importance of avoiding passion: marriage is "not by any to be enterprised, nor taken in hand, unadvisedly, lightly, or wantonly, to satisfy men's carnal lusts and appetites, like brute beasts that have no understanding; but reverently, discreetly, advisedly, soberly, and in the fear of God". The three reasons for marriage were "the procreation of children", "a remedy against sin, and to avoid fornication", and "the mutual society, help, and comfort, that the one ought to have of the other, both in prosperity and adversity". This last comes closest to a modern ideal of mutual love, but even here the careful language avoids any encouragement of excessive feeling. Celibacy was no longer required of the priesthood, and in theory virginity was no longer considered a higher calling than chaste married love, but medieval traditions were still strong culturally, and the ecclesiastical courts were active in their attempts to prevent premarital and extramarital sex.[2]

As well as religious teachings against "carnal lusts and appetites", there were economic forces acting against freedom of choice in marriage. Among property owners, marriage was in general "a collective decision of family and kin, not an individual one".[3] At the same time, the overall approach to it was both flexible and complex: "Instead of any clear-cut pattern of 'arranged' or 'free' marriages, a more subtle system prevailed in which love had a part to play in combination with prudential considerations, the pressures of community values, and (at middling- and upper-class levels) the interests of parents and sometimes other family members."[4]

Some of the plots of the plays make us well aware of the pressure of parents in arranged marriages: Juliet is promised by her father to the young Count Paris, just when she has found forbidden love with Romeo. There is ample documentary evidence from the time that arranged marriages were common among the nobility, and increasingly among the rising merchant class, as families cemented economic alliances. But the issue was not cut and dried. Advice books from the period stress the responsibility that parents have to ensure their children's happiness. Shakespeare found the story for his play in *Romeus and Juliet*, a long (and rather dull) poem by Arthur Brooke, who is clear about the issue of blame; in his epistle "To the Reader" he writes: "And to this end, good Reader, is this tragical matter written, to describe unto thee a couple of unfortunate lovers, thralling [imprisoning] themselves to unhonest desire; neglecting the authority and advice of parents and friends; conferring their principal counsels with drunken gossips and superstitious friars (the naturally fit instruments of unchastity); attempting all adventures of peril for the attaining of their wished lust . . . finally by all means of unhonest life hasting to most unhappy death."

The early scenes of Shakespeare's retelling of this story are close enough to the original, as the young men especially are shown to be irresponsible, and as Juliet's father urges Paris to be patient, and to win her love:

> But woo her, gentle Paris, get her heart,
> My will to her consent is but a part;
> And she agreed, within her scope of choice
> Lies my consent, and fair according voice. (1.2.15–18.)

Here Old Capulet balances admirably his ambition to make an advantageous match and his responsibility to ensure his daughter's happiness. These good intentions are forgotten, however, in the passions raised by Tybalt's death, and Juliet's unexpected refusal to obey him.

> An you be mine, I'll give you to my friend;
> An you be not, hang, beg, starve, die in the streets,
> For, by my soul, I'll ne'er acknowledge thee,
> Nor what is mine shall never do thee good. (3.5.192–5.)

Capulet's sudden change of heart, and the violence of his language, make clear Shakespeare's intention to complicate Brooke's simple moral, and to implicate the adult society with its feuds and its own excessive haste in the tragedy.

To compound the intensity of our response to the lovers, Shakespeare also stresses that Juliet is very young, not quite fourteen, and again we will be prompted to wonder whether this would have been seen as more the norm in Shakespeare's time. Recent research has shown without a doubt that the normal age for marriage in Shakespeare's time was as late as, or later than, in the twentieth century. The evidence, garnered from parish registries, is that most men and women married in their late twenties.[5] There was good reason for marrying late, since it took many years for those with less impressive resources than the Capulets to amass sufficient savings to permit setting up a household. Shakespeare's own marriage at the very young age of eighteen (to a woman a good eight years older) was exceptional and is usually explained by the early arrival of his first child, only six months after the wedding. An awareness of the social context of Shakespeare's day will modify our understanding of his approach to love; Shakespeare's choice of extreme youth for his tragic protagonists is clearly deliberate, and shocking. In this instance the sympathy a modern audience will feel for the lovers will be, in all probability, similar to the feelings of those privileged to see the original production, but we will take for granted a response that to them must have been far more radical, and correspondingly surprising.

Capulet's outburst at his daughter's resistance is also a reminder of the difference between Shakespeare's day and our own when it comes to the duty of obedience owed by the child to the parent, and the wife to the husband. Although Capulet's language is intemperate, there is no question that he must be obeyed. In Shakespeare, the most striking statement of this hierarchical and patriarchal social structure is Katherine's final speech in *The Taming of the Shrew*, where she eloquently draws parallels between domestic and national social structures:

Thy husband is thy lord, thy life, thy keeper,

> Thy head, thy sovereign; one that cares for thee . . .
>
> And craves no other tribute at thy hands
>
> But love, fair looks, and true obedience—
>
> Too little payment for so great a debt.
>
> Such duty as the subject owes the prince,
>
> Even such a woman oweth to her husband. (5.2.150–60.)

This passage is notoriously difficult for a modern audience to accept, or for an actor to perform. Is she deadly serious? Is it intended to be ironical? Has Petruchio's taming (we might think brainwashing) really been successful?

Whatever our critical response to Katherine's words, she enunciates a traditional position with admirable clarity. The wife must obey the husband, in precisely the same way that the subject was bound to obey the monarch. We must remember, however, that *The Taming of the Shrew* is an early work; when we compare Katherine and Petruchio with Shakespeare's later lovers Beatrice and Benedick from *Much Ado About Nothing,* we realize that what in Katherine is seen to be shrewishness in Beatrice becomes an admirable wit and strength of personality. That there is a debate concerning the level and appropriateness of male control in love is made very clear in *Othello*, when Desdemona and her attendant Emilia discuss Othello's erratic behaviour. Desdemona is idealistic – we might say almost masochistic – in her response to her husband: "even his stubbornness, his checks, his frowns . . . have grace and favour in them" (4.3.21–2). Emilia, however, argues passionately that women have the same feelings as their husbands and deserve the same respect:

> Let husbands know
>
> Their wives have sense like them; they see and smell,
>
> And have their palates both for sweet and sour,
>
> As husbands have.
>
> (4.3.96–9; see p.226, for the full passage.)[6]

Love in Renaissance literature

Emilia's trenchant comments may sound very modern, but Shakespeare's audience would have been familiar with literary attitudes to love that seem very foreign to us, and which bore very little relation to the social realities of marriage they would have seen around them. Writers in the late decades of the sixteenth century were excited by the sonnets of Petrarch, with their lyrics in praise of an ideal of feminine beauty. Sir Philip Sidney translated and adapted Petrarch in some of his sonnets in the great sequence *Astrophel and Stella*. To his loved one he writes:

> . . . not content to be perfection's heir
> Thyself dost strive all minds that way to move,
> Who mark in thee what is in thee most fair.
> So while thy beauty draws the heart to love,
> As fast thy virtue bends that love to good.

Sidney, however, finds the Petrarchan ideal difficult in practice; in the final line of the sonnet the writer reverses the direction of the praise: "But 'Ah,' Desire still cries, 'Give me some food!'". Shakespeare, in one of the best known of his sonnets written to the dark woman (or "Dark Lady"), exploits a similar transformation of the kind of idealized imagery associated with the tradition of courtly love: "My mistress' eyes are nothing like the sun" (130).

As Sidney's poem suggests, the tradition of courtly love itself was an attempt to convert the energy of erotic love into a spiritual quest. Baldessare Castiglione's influential text, *Libro del Cortegiano*, translated into English by Sir Thomas Hoby in 1561 as *The Book of the Courtier*, establishes the proposition that the love of a woman's beauty can lead through an ascending stair to an ultimate, spiritual, and transcendent love of beauty in the abstract. Castiglione's description of the lover fits well with the excesses of Shakespeare's young lovers, the men especially: "Because the influence of that beauty when it is present, giveth a wondrous delight to the lover, and setting his heart on fire, quickeneth and melteth certain virtues [which are] in a trance and congealed in the soul . . . Whereupon the soul taketh a delight, and with a certain wonder is aghast,[7] and yet enjoyeth she it, and (as it were) astonished together with the pleasure, feeleth the fear and reverence that men accustomably have toward holy matters, and thinketh herself to be in Paradise."[8]

In the early part of *Romeo and Juliet*, when Romeo thinks he is madly in love with the uncooperative Rosalind, he cheerfully spouts lines that combine many of the paradoxes so beloved of writers celebrating the ideals of courtly love:

> Love is a smoke made with the fume of sighs;
> Being purged, a fire sparkling in lovers' eyes;
> Being vexed, a sea nourished with lovers' tears.
> What is it else? A madness most discreet,
> A choking gall,[9] and a preserving sweet. (1.1.190–4.)

In this play it is the even younger Juliet who is acutely aware that fine language butters no bread. When she asks Romeo how he found her, his response is romantic, and impractical:

> With love's light wings did I o'erperch these walls,
> For stony limits cannot hold love out,
> And what love can do, that dares love attempt.
> Therefore thy kinsmen are no stop to me. (2.2.66–9)

– to which Juliet replies, far more sensibly, "If they do see thee, they will murder thee."

Juliet is not the only woman who is more pragmatic than her lover. In several of the comedies, Shakespeare makes it clear that the women have to educate their men, teaching them to discard the facile language of courtly love as they earn a maturity of judgement that will restrain the immediate and impatient erotic impulse of falling in love. In *As You Like It*, Orlando begins his exile in the Forest of Arden by papering the trees with love-sick, banal verses, which the clown Touchstone tellingly and bawdily parodies:

Sweetest nut hath sourest rind,

Such a nut is Rosalind.

He that sweetest rose will find

Must find love's prick and Rosalind. (3.2.105–8.)

The subject of his adulation, Rosalind, sets to work to educate Orlando in the more prosaic realities of mutual love (see pp.182–5).

The problem with the idealization expressed in the language of courtly love is that it fails to recognize the genuine humanity of the women it describes, and too readily leads to its diametric opposite, misogyny, as the object of love inevitably falls short of the ideal. Shakespeare's tragedies of love, and the group of plays known as the "problem plays", confront this reality.

Moderation and excess in love

In his poems, and in both comedy and tragedy, Shakespeare makes clear his awareness of the power of sexual love, capable at any moment of overtaking reasonable behaviour in men and women. It is one of Shakespeare's early clowns, Bottom in *A Midsummer Night's Dream*, who most trenchantly puts it. Titania, under the influence of Oberon's magic, sees Bottom and falls instantly in love with him: "thy fair virtue's force perforce doth move me / On the first view to say, to swear, I love thee"; Bottom's response is splendidly accurate: "Methinks, mistress, you should have little reason for that. And yet, to say the truth, reason and love keep little company together nowadays" (3.1.135–9). In this play the magic juice that Puck applies to Titania's (and others') eyes provides a conveniently objective cause for falling in love at first sight. Rapidity of emotional response is clearly convenient within the brief compass of a play, where the plot must hum along, but Shakespeare is not alone in writing about the suddenness of sexual attraction; in *As You Like It*, the love-struck Phoebe quotes Marlowe's famous dictum: "Dead shepherd, now I find thy saw [saying] of might: / Who ever loved that loved not at first sight?" (3.5.80–81). The quotation is typically Shakespearean in its irony, since Phoebe has fallen in love with Rosalind's male disguise. Sudden love may not be as absurd as Phoebe's (we do not dismiss Romeo and Juliet so readily), but it is clearly in need of restraint, since it enters in the eye, and is thus influenced by the surface rather than the heart.

One of the many tensions in love is thus the need to control the excesses of passion that love so readily leads to. The late sonnet probably written to the dark woman, "Th'expense of spirit in a waste of shame" (sonnet 129), makes clear the potentially destructive effect of passion, in this case "lust in action", which is

> Past reason hunted, and no sooner had,
>
> Past reason hated as a swallowed bait
>
> On purpose laid to make the taker mad.

From his earliest to his final works, Shakespeare dramatizes the consequent battle between celebrating the joy and freedom of love (where the bond of marriage finally permits freedom of sexual expression), and the need to restrain excess. Nowhere is this tension clearer than in the paradoxical moment where passion teeters on a knife-edge between love and jealousy; fear that what the eye sees is not what the heart feels. The disjunction between eye and heart echoes through the sonnets, as the "I" of the poem attempts to reconcile the external beauty of his loved ones with behaviour that results in pain. In the plays, the male eye at one moment sees his lover's warmth as a positive affirmation of love; at the next, confirmation of excessive sexual heat. After all, to be chaste was to be associated with white and with cold, as Hamlet warns Ophelia: "be thou as chaste as ice, as pure as snow, thou shalt not escape calumny[10]" (3.1.137–8).

In *Othello*, Iago homes in on Desdemona's obvious strength of feeling, suggesting that it is a sign of sexual promiscuity. To begin with, Othello defends her:

> 'Tis not to make me jealous
>
> To say my wife is fair, feeds well, loves company,
>
> Is free of speech, sings, plays, and dances well;
>
> Where virtue is, these are more virtuous. (3.3.197–200)

Yet when he next holds her hand he is convinced that this same freedom of expression is excessively liberal, and the mere fact that she is a living, breathing woman becomes evidence against her:

OTHELLO   Give me your hand. This hand is moist, my lady.

DESDEMONA   It yet hath felt no age nor known no sorrow.

OTHELLO   This argues fruitfulness and liberal heart.

            Hot, hot, and moist. This hand of yours requires

            A sequester [isolation] from liberty, feasting and

              prayer. (3.4.36–40)

In this world there is no room for moderation between extremes: the woman is viewed as either hot and licentious, or cold and chaste. This attitude was one with a long pedigree in the well-attested tradition of misogyny in the teachings of the Church, whether Catholic or Protestant.[11] Several of Shakespeare's tragic protagonists tend at times of crisis to attack women in general: Hamlet's attack on Ophelia, Lear's madness on the heath, and the pervasive suspicion of female sexuality that permeates the problem plays. Even in the comedies, a stock figure of fun was the cuckold, a man who had insufficient control over his wife, such that she had been unfaithful to him.

Control is one response to the anxiety that comes from the perceived slipperiness of love and the threat of loose or intemperate behaviour. Most notoriously, Petruchio, in *The Taming of the Shrew*, institutes a regime of masculine domination, taking as his inspiration the process of taming a hawk for the sport of hunting. The soliloquy where he announces his plan is full of hawking imagery: the falcon "stoops" when it swoops upon its prey, the "lure" the reward for returning to the trainer, a "haggard" is an adult female hawk as yet untamed, to "watch" is to keep the bird awake, and a captive bird "bates" when it flies and struggles against the cage, beating its wings:

> My falcon now is sharp and passing empty.
> And till she stoop she must not be full-gorg'd,
> For then she never looks upon her lure.
> Another way I have to man my haggard,
> To make her come, and know her keeper's call,
> That is, to watch her, as we watch these kites
> That bate and beat, and will not be obedient.
> She ate no meat to-day, nor none shall eat;
> Last night she slept not, nor to-night she shall not . . .
> Ay, and amid this hurly I intend
> That all is done in reverend care of her . . .
> This is a way to kill a wife with kindness,
> And thus I'll curb her mad and headstrong humour.
> (4.1.178–97)

A modern reader will feel uncomfortable or indignant at this deliberate objectification and subjugation of the woman,[12] even though Shakespeare gives her considerable wit and spirit. There is some reassurance in the comedies, where the women are given power over the men; in *Love's Labour's Lost*, for example, the queen and her three attendant ladies resist the obvious comic ending – as the Lord Berowne remarks, "Our wooing doth not end like an old play: / Jack hath not Jill" (5.2.872–3). The men must earn their love by undertaking tasks for a full year before marriage can be considered (see pp.153–5).

The debate between the need for control and freedom to express the vitality of love continues throughout Shakespeare's career. One of the more puzzling of the sonnets suggests that the ideal lover is impassive, even cold and distant:

> They that have power to hurt, and will do none,

That do not do the thing they most do show,

Who, moving others, are themselves as stone,

Unmoved, cold, and to temptation slow:

They rightly do inherit heaven's graces . . . (sonnet 94)

And the late play *The Tempest* is structured around a central figure, Prospero, who exercises rigorous control over the young lovers Ferdinand and Miranda, insisting that they restrain their passion for each other until they are safely wed.[13] Prospero's language has the effect of reducing their love to a commercial transaction, and his warning against premarital sex is bitter:

Then, as my gift, and thine own acquisition

Worthily purchased, take my daughter. But

If thou dost break her virgin-knot before

All sanctimonious ceremonies may

With full and holy rite be ministered,

No sweet aspersion [shower] shall the heavens let fall

To make this contract grow; but barren hate,

Sour-eyed disdain, and discord, shall bestrew

The union of your bed with weeds so loathly

That you shall hate it both. (4.1.13–22)

Another late play, *The Winter's Tale*, provides a welcome counterbalance to this rigidity of control. In the early part of the play, King Leontes is overcome with irrational jealousy, suspecting that his pregnant wife, Hermione, has been unfaithful with his childhood friend, Polixenes. His actions are disastrous, and bring the play to the brink of tragedy; like Othello, he interprets his wife's vitality as excessive heat; like Othello, his actions bring destruction to his happiness. But this plot moves past tragedy into a kind of redemption, where in a final scene he confronts Hermione's statue:

O, thus she stood,

Even with such life of majesty—warm life,

As now it coldly stands—when first I wooed her.

I am ashamed. Does not the stone rebuke me

For being more stone than it? (5.3.34–8)

He has come to understand that Hermione's liveliness was the warmth of love, not sexual heat; a glad and fertile mean between frigidity and licence. Similarly, the young loves of Perdita and Florizel in the same play provide a balance, as they choose to wait for marriage to consummate their love, at the same time expressing it freely (see pp.248–50).

The balance between excess and control is never sure, and even when it is gained, the pleasures of love seem as fleeting as the beauty of a rose (always threatened with the canker-worm) or a summer's day (see sonnets 35, 54, 18). Not only does love fade, but it threatens to turn sour the moment it is achieved:

The sweets we wish for turn to loathèd sours

Even in the moment that we call them ours.

(*The Rape of Lucrece* 697–8.)

This fear is echoed many times in the selections in this volume, especially in the frequency with which Shakespeare has his characters recall the great and tragic myths of Greece where lovers proved their passion through meeting a sticky end: Troilus and Cressida, Hero and Leander, Dido and Aeneas. And of course today we will add the couple made famous by Shakespeare, Romeo and Juliet. In the sonnets, especially, Shakespeare's verse is haunted by the destructive hand of Time as it transforms flourishing youth to wrinkled age:

Time doth transfix the flourish set on youth,

And delves the parallels in beauty's brow;

Feeds on the rarities of nature's truth,

And nothing stands but for his scythe to mow. (sonnet 60)

The sonnets claim, with varying confidence, that there is an antidote for the transience of beauty and love – the art of poetry itself. In the plays the exploration is more equivocal; plays end conveniently, loose ends generally tidied up. Romeo and Juliet will have statues erected in their honour, as their families vow to end their feud (but compete for whose statue will be the more expensive); couples in the comedies marry, are able to consummate their love with the blessing of the church, and the plays end conveniently before the long struggle of marriage begins. There are few married couples in the plays (see pp.176–7 for the tense interaction between the newlyweds Jessica and Lorenzo in *The Merchant of Venice*).

Just occasionally Shakespeare gives a hint of a different antidote to the passing of love, one which seems to depend on the willingness of the woman to keep the game alive. In *As You Like It*, Rosalind imagines life after marriage, and fears that her lover will lose interest: "men are April when they woo, December when they wed. Maids are May when they are maids, but the sky changes when they are wives" (4.1.138–41). Her answer is to be forever changeable, forever challenging: "I will be more jealous of thee than a Barbary cock-pigeon over his hen, more clamorous than a parrot against rain, more new-fangled [fascinated by novelty] than an ape, more giddy in my desires than a monkey" (141–43). A wise wife will be always contrary, "The wiser the waywarder" (153). In the great tragedy of married love and the destinies of empires, *Antony and Cleopatra*, Cleopatra is imagined as always teasing, always manipulating, always new; forever making "hungry / Where most she satisfies" (2.2.247–8). *As You Like It* ends with marriage, so we never see how successful Rosalind will be; and Cleopatra's contrariness leads at the end to the deaths of both lovers.

Poet and playwright

There is inevitably much omitted in this short discussion of Shakespeare's almost infinite variety in creating lovers and the language of love. The love of parents for children (especially, in the later plays, the father for the daughter); self-love (although the young friend in the sonnets seems at times narcissistic); and the love of God, represented directly in one sonnet, and indirectly in the lovers who make of their human love a kind of idolatry (see *Romeo and Juliet*, and sonnets 146 and 105).

As we read Shakespeare, we are continually reminded that he was both a wordsmith and a dramatist, both a poet and a writer who depended on the audience to pay to see and hear his plays. There is a tension between these two vocations: words can hold up action, and action can stifle words. Two of Shakespeare's major tragic protagonists are caught in precisely this dilemma: Hamlet and Macbeth both speak when they should act and act when they should be talking or thinking. In the early plays, especially, the action is periodically put on hold while a character speaks what is in effect a brilliant aria; even in the later plays we are asked to listen to Jacques on the seven ages of man, Hamlet's soliloquies, or Prospero's decision to abjure his magic arts. Film treatments of Shakespeare tend to be impatient with this kind of verbal richness; film replaces gorgeousness of language with colourful cinematography and special effects. On stage, actors have the luxury of creating depth of character and atmosphere with the words Shakespeare has given them.

When he was writing poems specifically for the page rather than the stage, Shakespeare seized the opportunity for words to take preeminence. At the same time he remains the dramatist: he adds drama to the story of Venus and Adonis that he inherited from Ovid, and even in the cramped space of the fourteen-line sonnet, he continually introduces dramatic reversals and paradoxes. Shakespeare did not write an Ovid-like "art of love", but his works collectively provide illumination and insight; like the changing fire of an opal, he gives us words to express the range and depth of human passion in all its colours.

WILLIAM SHAKESPEARE

PART ONE
Poems

1

The Sonnets

Shakespeare's sonnets offer a fascinating array of explorations into the passions and tensions of love; at the same time, they are deeply puzzling. We do not with any certainty know when they were written; who they were written to; or what audience Shakespeare intended for them. The best guess is that they are the products of Shakespeare's more mature years, written intermittently, and very possibly revised or polished over time. There is no clear evidence either that the publication of the poems was approved by Shakespeare or that they were in some way published without his consent.

The cast

Who they were written to has caused "much throwing about of brains" (Guildenstern's phrase). The issue is complicated by the desire of many to find autobiographical information in the poems. There do seem to be four characters hovering behind the lines: the writer, a young friend, a rival poet, and a woman of dark hair and complexion. She is traditionally called the Dark Lady, but I shall refer to her as the dark woman, since I can find no indication of higher rank in the poems, and the writer's judgement of her is that she is certainly no lady in behaviour. The rival could be any one of a dozen brilliant poets in a brilliant period. The major puzzle that writers on the sonnets love to argue about is the friend. He is young, exceptionally beautiful – almost feminine in looks – and there are some indications that he comes from a somewhat higher social class than the writer. There is no space here to explore the different theories as to his identity:[1] most critics assume that he is aristocratic, on the basis of one or two poems in which the writer seems servile, or appears to ask for a patron. The problem is that Shakespeare takes rather naturally to poetic images, and it is impossible to tell whether he is speaking of literal or metaphorical servitude or patronage. The question is complicated by the enigmatic dedication to the sonnets, apparently devised by their printer, Thomas Thorpe. Who is "THE.ONLIE.BEGETTER" he mentions? The most natural interpretation would be the writer of the poems. But the initials are "W.H."; some scholars have suggested that this is a misprint for "W.SH." or "W.S." and that the begetter is William Shakespeare. Alternatively, the begetter may be rather more mundane – the person who provided the manuscript to the printer; several candidates have been suggested. The most seductive alternative is that W.H. was an aristocratic patron of Shakespeare's. But there is at least one significant problem: the dedication is to "Mr." – Master – W.H. The term "master" denotes a gentleman, certainly, but it would be insulting to apply it to a member of the higher nobility.

The remaining member of this modest cast of four is the writer. In the most obvious way this is Shakespeare; but we are reminded when we read the poems of contemporaries like John Donne that poets of the time tended to create personas or characters to speak their verse – and Shakespeare was adept at precisely this activity in his plays. Some of the poems certainly seem to create a persona of someone who is substantially older than Shakespeare could have been in a literal sense; the wonderful sonnet 73 ("That time of year thou may'st in me behold") is a good example. As we read the sonnets, however, we become aware of a powerful presence in the first person pronoun ("I", "me", "mine"), one that speaks to us in a more personal way than a more distant persona or a character in a play.[2] In other words, Shakespeare's personal voice is there, but dramatized to varying degrees in the different sonnets.

The plot

If in the sonnets Shakespeare is being, at least to some extent, the dramatist, what is the plot behind the sonnet sequence? The order in which they are printed seems to divide them into two unequal parts: 126 addressed to the young friend, and 38 to the dark woman. However, nothing is certain; this division has been both defended and attacked. The opening is straightforward: there is a young man, a friend, who is reluctant to marry, and the writer is urging him to do so as a way of making his beauty more permanent. But the poems rapidly move onto other topics. Later events seem to involve betrayals of some kind by both the friend and the writer, and in both sections of the sequence there is a suggestion that the friend and the dark woman may have had an affair. While it is tempting to connect the dots in order to make a coherent story, the dots are very far apart. I am reminded of the way that imagined patterns in the stars make up very different constellations in different cultures: "in the night, imagining some fear, / How easy is a bush supposed a bear?" (*A Midsummer Night's Dream*, 5.1.21–2).

Whatever the events that lie behind the poems, it is clear that Shakespeare used them as a starting point for meditating on images and emotions. Some short sequences of two or three poems are clearly interconnected, and could be read as double or triple sonnets (set out here on the same pages), but for the most part the effect is more of a stream of consciousness than a narrative; if in some magic way we could suddenly find out exactly what was supposed to have happened, and who was addressed, the effect on the meaning or feeling expressed in the poems would be minimal.

Audience: the language of love

More interesting is the question of the wider audience for whom Shakespeare was writing. Time and again the poems proclaim that they will be the means of providing immortality for their subject, as readers – like us – return to the poems in later times. The language of the sonnets presupposes an audience of sophistication, interested in intricate images and capable of disentangling a syntax that is sometimes contorted, even "opaque".[3] Shakespeare was writing at the end of a long tradition of sonnet sequences, so he could assume that his audience was familiar with its form and conventions. The sonnet is an elegant but demanding medium; after the full orchestral effects Shakespeare had available to him in the theatre, the sonnet must have seemed Procrustean in its limitations: all thoughts must be squeezed into fourteen lines, with rigorous sub-groupings of four, and a final couplet that must somehow sound an ending without being trite. Shakespeare was well aware of the difficulty of saying something new:

> If there be nothing new, but that which is
> Hath been before, how are our brains beguiled,
> Which, labouring for invention, bear amiss
> The second burden of a former child? (sonnet 59)

He may have felt the burden of originality greater in these poems than in his plays, where he was perfectly happy to rewrite old stories for new audiences. Poetry makes very different demands on the writer; if the habitual mode of the plays is irony, as those on stage seldom know as much as the audience, the typical mode of the sonnets is paradox. The writer's mistress is unconventional, "nothing like the sun" (130); the beauty of a summer's day is far too fragile to be a suitable comparison to his loved one's beauty (18); more darkly, there is the possibility in the loved one of "lascivious grace" (40), a single phrase that startlingly juxtaposes the ugly and the delicate.

Nowhere is the paradox implied in the dissonance between outward beauty (as seen by the eye) and inward beauty (as figured in the heart) more keenly felt than in the short second section of the sonnets, associated with the dark woman. The mood in these sonnets shifts abruptly from one to the next – from witty delight to angry disgust – and there are no shorter sequences of poems connected to one another. This section also includes the one sonnet that meditates directly upon religion (146, "Poor soul, the centre of my sinful earth"), and three that are very probably from an earlier period (145, 153, 154). Possibly because there are so few poems in this section, the reader's sense of the writer's relationship to the dark woman is much more of an emotional roller-coaster than those addressed to the young friend.

Modern readers may well be less troubled than those of earlier times that the writer is so clearly attracted to the physical appearance of his young friend. The most striking sonnet in this context is the one where the writer confronts this fact directly:

A woman's face with Nature's own hand painted

Hast thou, the master mistress of my passion. (20)

The sonnet contrasts "false" women with the steadfast personality and natural beauty of the friend and ends with the rueful observation that Nature's addition of one thing – the friend's penis – robs him of the opportunity to consummate his love. This complex poem works, as so often the sonnets do, in seemingly contradictory directions: the physical nature of the love is affirmed at the same time as it is denied. This capacity to propose a position on the matter of love, and immediately to modify it, is consistent throughout the sonnets, partly, no doubt, because of that fourteen-line structure with the built-in expectation of surprise after eight or twelve lines. But a further, perhaps unexpected, aspect of the poems is that the majority have no specific indication of gender at all. For this reason, the wonderful sonnet 18 ("Shall I compare thee to a summer's day") turns up happily in Valentine cards despite its location in the section of the sonnets presumably addressed to the friend. And the passionate and troubled denunciation of lust in sonnet 129 ("Th'expense of spirit in a waste of shame") is not specifically addressed to anyone, so that to assign it to the dark woman is to assume guilt by association. In each case, the individual sonnet can both be appreciated in isolation, and be seen to become more complex when it is contextualized. Shakespeare's frequent avoidance of the personal pronoun has the effect of ensuring that the sonnets as a whole reach toward a more generalized sense of the nature of love – its strengths, and its manifold weaknesses and challenges. The effect of the androgynous young friend is similar to that of Adonis, in *Venus and Adonis*, and, in the plays, the boy actors dressed as young women (then sometimes disguised as boys); Bruce Smith accurately remarks that in these figures desire "flow[s] out in all directions toward all the sexual objects that beckon in the romantic landscape".[4] It is an instructive exercise to imagine switching the addressee of some of these potentially neutral sonnets from male to female, or female to male. To do so is to connect the dots in different, and potentially enlightening ways.[5]

Whether we mentally reorder the sonnets or not, one major motif that returns again and again as we read them is the writer's profound awareness of the fragility of both beauty and love. The friend's beauty will no more last than a summer's day, though the lines that record this melancholy fact may survive as long as men can breathe or eyes can see (18). Even the sonnet most often quoted as a triumphant statement of permanence in love is steeped in an awareness of the inevitability of change (116). It begins confidently enough: "Let me not to the marriage of true minds / Admit impediments", but the whole point is that time causes everything around it to change, most particularly beauty, where "rosy lips and cheeks" come within the circle of time's reaping sickle. And the other sonnets tend to be less optimistic about even one fixed point in the turning world of love; many compelling sonnets speak of the fragility of the defence that art and love try to build against "the wrackful siege of batt'ring days" (65). It is not surprising, then, that the writer returns continually to the realization that "everything that grows / Holds in perfection but a little moment" (15). The sonnets meditate upon this inevitable, if unpalatable truth; the plays, in the second section of this book, dramatize it.

1[1]

From fairest creatures we desire increase,[2]
That thereby beauty's rose might never die,
But as the riper[3] should by time decease
His tender heir might bear his memory:
But thou, contracted[4] to thine own bright eyes,
Feed'st thy light's flame with self-substantial[5] fuel,
Making a famine where abundance lies,
Thyself thy foe, to thy sweet self too cruel.
Thou that art now the world's fresh ornament,
And only herald to the gaudy spring,
Within thine own bud buriest thy content,[6]
And, tender churl, mak'st waste in niggarding.[7]
　　Pity the world, or else this glutton be,
　　To eat the world's due, by the grave and thee.[8]

2

When forty winters shall besiege thy brow,
And dig deep trenches in thy beauty's field,[1]
Thy youth's proud livery,[2] so gazed on now,
Will be a tattered weed of small worth held:
Then being asked, where all thy beauty lies,
Where all the treasure of thy lusty days,
To say, within thine own deep-sunken eyes,
Were an all-eating shame, and thriftless praise.
How much more praise deserved thy beauty's use[3]
If thou couldst answer, "This fair child of mine
Shall sum my count, and make my old excuse",[4]
Proving his beauty by succession[5] thine.
　　This were to be new made when thou art old,
　　And see thy blood warm when thou feel'st it cold.

3

Look in thy glass,[1] and tell the face thou viewest,
Now is the time that face should form another,
Whose fresh repair,[2] if now thou not renewest,
Thou dost beguile[3] the world, unbless some mother.
For where is she so fair whose uneared[4] womb
Disdains the tillage of thy husbandry?[5]
Or who is he so fond will be the tomb
Of his self-love, to stop posterity?
Thou art thy mother's glass, and she in thee
Calls back the lovely April of her prime;
So thou through windows of thine age[6] shalt see,
Despite of wrinkles, this thy golden time.
    But if thou live remembered not to be,
      Die single, and thine image dies with thee.

4

Unthrifty loveliness, why dost thou spend
Upon thyself thy beauty's legacy?[1]
Nature's bequest gives nothing, but doth lend,
And, being frank,[2] she lends to those are free.
Then, beauteous niggard, why dost thou abuse
The bounteous largesse given thee to give?
Profitless usurer,[3] why dost thou use
So great a sum of sums, yet canst not live?
For having traffic[4] with thyself alone,
Thou of thyself thy sweet self dost deceive;
Then how, when nature calls thee to be gone,
What acceptable audit canst thou leave?
    Thy unused beauty must be tombed with thee,
      Which used, lives th'executor to be.

5[1]

Those hours[2] that with gentle work did frame
The lovely gaze where every eye doth dwell
Will play the tyrants to the very same,
And that unfair[3] which fairly doth excel.
For never-resting time leads summer on
To hideous winter, and confounds[4] him there,
Sap checked with frost and lusty leaves quite gone,
Beauty o'er-snowed and bareness everywhere;
Then were not summer's distillation[5] left
A liquid prisoner pent[6] in walls of glass,
Beauty's effect with beauty were bereft,
Nor it, nor no remembrance what it was.
    But flowers distilled, though they with winter meet,
    Lose but their show; their substance still lives sweet.

6

Then let not winter's ragged hand deface
In thee thy summer ere thou be distilled:
Make sweet some vial;[1] treasure thou some place
With beauty's treasure ere it be self-killed.
That use is not forbidden usury[2]
Which happies those that pay the willing loan;
That's for thyself to breed another thee,
Or ten times happier be it ten for one;
Ten times thyself were happier than thou art,
If ten of thine ten times refigured thee;
Then what could death do if thou shouldst depart,
Leaving thee living in posterity?
    Be not self-willed, for thou art much too fair
    To be death's conquest and make worms thine heir.

7

Lo, in the Orient[1] when the gracious light[2]
Lifts up his burning head, each under eye[3]
Doth homage to his new-appearing sight,
Serving[4] with looks his sacred majesty;
And having climbed the steep-up heavenly hill,[5]
Resembling strong youth in his middle age,
Yet mortal looks adore his beauty still,
Attending on his golden pilgrimage:
But when from highmost pitch with weary car,
Like feeble age he reeleth from the day,
The eyes, fore-duteous, now converted are
From his low tract, and look another way:
    So thou, thyself out-going in thy noon,
      Unlooked on diest, unless thou get a son.

8

Music to hear,[1] why hear'st thou music sadly?
Sweets with sweets war not, joy delights in joy;
Why lov'st thou that which thou receiv'st not gladly,
Or else receiv'st with pleasure thine annoy?[2]
If the true concord of well-tunèd sounds
By unions married, do offend thine ear,
They do but sweetly chide thee, who confounds
In singleness the parts that thou shouldst bear:[3]
Mark how one string, sweet husband to another,
Strikes each in each by mutual ordering,[4]
Resembling sire, and child, and happy mother,
Who all in one, one pleasing note do sing:
    Whose speechless song being many, seeming one,[5]
      Sings this to thee: 'Thou single wilt prove none.'

9

Is it for fear to wet a widow's eye
That thou consum'st thyself in single life?
Ah, if thou issueless¹ shalt hap to die,
The world will wail thee like a mateless wife;
The world will be thy widow, and still² weep
That thou no form of thee hast left behind,
When every private³ widow well may keep,
By children's eyes, her husband's shape in mind:
Look what an unthrift in the world doth spend,
Shifts but his place, for still the world enjoys it;⁴
But beauty's waste hath in the world an end,
And kept unused the user so destroys it:
    No love toward others in that bosom sits
    That on himself such murd'rous shame commits.

10

For shame deny that thou bear'st love to any,
Who for thyself art so unprovident.
Grant, if thou wilt, thou art beloved of many,
But that thou none lov'st is most evident:
For thou art so possessed with murd'rous hate,
That 'gainst thyself thou stick'st¹ not to conspire,
Seeking that beauteous roof² to ruinate
Which to repair should be thy chief desire:
Oh, change thy thought, that I may change my mind;
Shall hate be fairer lodged than gentle love?
Be as thy presence is, gracious and kind,
Or to thyself at least kind-hearted prove;
    Make thee another self for love of me,
    That beauty still may live in thine or thee.

11

As fast as thou shalt wane, so fast thou grow'st
In one of thine, from that which thou departest;
And that fresh blood which youngly thou bestow'st
Thou mayst call thine, when thou from youth convertest.
Herein lives wisdom, beauty, and increase;
Without this, folly, age, and cold decay.
If all were minded so, the times should cease,
And threescore year would make the world away:[1]
Let those whom nature hath not made for store,
Harsh, featureless, and rude, barrenly perish;
Look whom she best endowed, she gave the more;
Which bounteous gift thou shouldst in bounty cherish:
 She carved thee for her seal,[2] and meant thereby
 Thou shouldst print more, not let that copy die.

12

When I do count the clock that tells the time,
And see the brave[1] day sunk in hideous night;
When I behold the violet past prime,
And sable[2] curls all silvered o'er with white:
When lofty trees I see barren of leaves,
Which erst[3] from heat did canopy the herd,
And summer's green all girded[4] up in sheaves
Borne on the bier[5] with white and bristly beard:[6]
Then of thy beauty do I question make,
That thou among the wastes of time must go,
Since sweets and beauties do themselves forsake,
And die as fast as they see others grow,
 And nothing 'gainst Time's scythe can make defence,
 Save breed,[7] to brave[8] him when he takes thee hence.

13

Oh that you were yourself! But, love, you are
No longer yours than you yourself here[1] live.
Against this coming end you should prepare,
And your sweet semblance to some other give.
So should that beauty which you hold in lease
Find no determination;[2] then you were
Yourself again after yourself's decease,
When your sweet issue your sweet form should bear.
Who lets so fair a house fall to decay,
Which husbandry[3] in honour might uphold
Against the stormy gusts of winter's day
And barren rage of death's eternal cold?
    Oh, none but unthrifts, dear my love you know:
    You had a father; let your son say so.

14

Not from the stars do I my judgement pluck,[1]
And yet methinks I have astronomy;
But not to tell of good or evil luck,
Of plagues, of dearths,[2] or seasons' quality;
Nor can I fortune to brief minutes tell,[3]
'Pointing[4] to each his thunder, rain and wind,
Or say with princes if it shall go well
By oft predict[5] that I in heaven find.
But from thine eyes my knowledge I derive,
And, constant stars, in them I read such art
As truth and beauty shall together thrive
If from thyself, to store[6] thou wouldst convert:
    Or else of thee this I prognosticate,
    Thy end is truth's and beauty's doom and date.

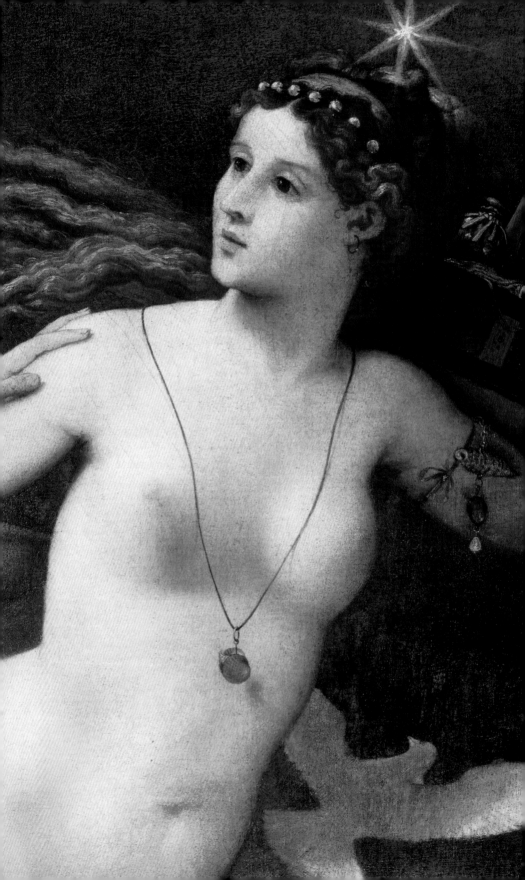

15[1]

When I consider everything that grows
Holds in perfection but a little moment;
That this huge stage[2] presenteth naught but shows
Whereon the stars in secret influence comment;
When I perceive that men as plants increase,
Cheered and checked[3] even by the self-same sky,
Vaunt in their youthful sap, at height decrease,
And wear their brave[4] state out of memory;
Then the conceit[5] of this inconstant stay
Sets you, most rich in youth, before my sight,
Where wasteful time debateth[6] with decay
To change your day of youth to sullied night;
    And all in war with Time for love of you,
    As he takes from you, I engraft you new.

16

But wherefore do not you a mightier way
Make war upon this bloody tyrant, Time,
And fortify yourself in your decay
With means more blessed than my barren[1] rhyme?
Now stand you on the top of happy hours,
And many maiden gardens, yet unset,[2]
With virtuous wish would bear your living flowers,
Much liker than your painted counterfeit:[3]
So should the lines of life that life repair,
Which this, Time's pencil, or my pupil pen,
Neither in inward worth nor outward fair,
Can make you live yourself in eyes of men.
    To give away yourself, keeps yourself still,
    And you must live drawn by your own sweet skill.[4]

17

Who will believe my verse in time to come,
If it were filled with your most high deserts?
Though yet, heaven knows, it is but as a tomb
Which hides your life, and shows not half your parts:
If I could write the beauty of your eyes,
And in fresh numbers[1] number all your graces,
The age to come would say, "This poet lies:
Such heavenly touches ne'er touched earthly faces."
So should my papers (yellowed with their age)
Be scorned, like old men of less truth than tongue,[2]
And your true rights be termed a poet's rage,
And strètched metre[3] of an antique song.
    But were some child of yours alive that time,
    You should live twice: in it, and in my rhyme.

18[1]

Shall I compare thee to a summer's day?
Thou art more lovely and more temperate:
Rough winds do shake the darling buds of May,
And summer's lease[2] hath all too short a date:
Sometime too hot the eye of heaven[3] shines,
And often is his gold complexion dimmed;
And every fair from fair sometime[4] declines,
By chance, or nature's changing course untrimmed:[5]
But thy eternal summer shall not fade,
Nor lose possession of that fair thou ow'st,
Nor shall death brag thou wander'st in his shade,
When in eternal lines to time thou grow'st:
    So long as men can breathe or eyes can see,
    So long lives this, and this gives life to thee.

19

Devouring Time, blunt thou the lion's paws,
And make the earth devour her own sweet brood;
Pluck the keen teeth from the fierce tiger's jaws,
And burn the long-lived Phoenix[1] in her blood;
Make glad and sorry seasons as thou fleet'st,
And do whate'er thou wilt, swift-footed Time,
To the wide world and all her fading sweets:
But I forbid thee one most heinous crime,
Oh, carve not with thy hours my love's fair brow,
Nor draw no lines there with thine antique[2] pen;
Him in thy course untainted[3] do allow
For beauty's pattern to succeeding men.
    Yet do thy worst, old Time: despite thy wrong,
    My love shall in my verse ever live young.

20[1]

A woman's face with Nature's own hand painted[2]
Hast thou, the master mistress[3] of my passion;
A woman's gentle heart, but not acquainted
With shifting change, as is false women's fashion;
An eye more bright than theirs, less false in rolling,
Gilding the object whereupon it gazeth;[4]
A man in hue all hues in his controlling,[5]
Which steals men's eyes and women's souls amazeth;
And for a woman wert thou first created,
Till nature as she wrought thee fell a-doting,
And by addition me of thee defeated,
By adding one thing to my purpose nothing.[6]
    But since she pricked thee out[7] for women's pleasure,
    Mine be thy love, and thy love's use their treasure.[8]

21

So is it not with me as with that Muse,[1]
Stirred by a painted[2] beauty to his verse,
Who heaven itself for ornament doth use,
And every fair with his fair doth rehearse,[3]
Making a couplement of proud compare
With sun and moon, with earth and sea's rich gems;
With April's first-born flowers, and all things rare
That heaven's air in this huge rondure[4] hems.
Oh, let me true in love but truly write,
And then believe me: my love is as fair
As any mother's child, though not so bright
As those gold candles fixed in heaven's air:[5]
    Let them say more that like of hearsay[6] well,
    I will not praise, that purpose not to sell.

22

My glass[1] shall not persuade me I am old,
So long as youth and thou are of one date;[2]
But when in thee time's furrows I behold,
Then look I death my days should expiate.[3]
For all that beauty that doth cover thee
Is but the seemly raiment of my heart,
Which in thy breast doth live, as thine in me;[4]
How can I then be elder than thou art?
Oh, therefore love be of thyself so wary,
As I not for myself, but for thee will,[5]
Bearing thy heart, which I will keep so chary[6]
As tender nurse her babe from faring ill.
    Presume not on thy heart when mine is slain;
    Thou gav'st me thine not to give back again.[7]

23

As an unperfect actor on the stage,
Who with his fear is put besides his part;[1]
Or some fierce thing replete with too much rage,
Whose strength's abundance weakens his own heart;[2]
So I, for fear of trust,[3] forget to say
The perfect ceremony of love's right,
And in mine own love's strength seem to decay,
O'ercharged with burden of mine own love's might:
Oh, let my books[4] be then the eloquence,
And dumb presagers[5] of my speaking breast,
Who plead for love, and look for recompense,
More than that tongue that more hath more expressed.
    Oh, learn to read what silent love hath writ!
    To hear with eyes belongs to love's fine wit.

24

Mine eye hath played the painter, and hath steeled[1]
Thy beauty's form in table of my heart;
My body is the frame wherein 'tis held,
And perspective it is best painter's art;
For through the painter must you see his skill,
To find where your true image pictured lies,
Which in my bosom's shop is hanging still,
That hath his windows glazèd with thine eyes:
Now see what good turns eyes for eyes have done:
Mine eyes have drawn thy shape, and thine for me
Are windows to my breast, wherethrough the sun
Delights to peep, to gaze therein on thee;
    Yet eyes this cunning want[2] to grace their art:
    They draw but what they see, know not the heart.

25

Let those who are in favour with their stars
Of public honour and proud titles boast,
Whilst I, whom fortune of such triumph bars,
Unlooked for[1] joy in that I honour most.
Great princes' favourites their fair leaves spread
But as the marigold at the sun's eye,
And in themselves their pride lies buried,
For at a frown they in their glory die.
The painful[2] warrior famousèd for worth,
After a thousand victories once foiled,
Is from the book of honour razèd[3] quite,
And all the rest forgot for which he toiled:
    Then happy I, that love and am beloved
    Where I may not remove, nor be removed.

26[1]

Lord of my love, to whom in vassalage[2]
Thy merit hath my duty strongly knit:
To thee I send this written embassage[3]
To witness duty, not to show my wit;
Duty so great, which wit so poor as mine
May make seem bare, in wanting words to show it;
But that I hope some good conceit[4] of thine
In thy soul's thought, all naked, will bestow it.[5]
Till whatsoever star that guides my moving
Points on me graciously with fair aspect,[6]
And puts apparel on my tattered loving,
To show me worthy of thy sweet respect:
    Then may I dare to boast how I do love thee;
    Till then, not show my head where thou mayst prove me.[7]

27[1]

Weary with toil, I haste me to my bed,

The dear repose for limbs with travel[2] tired;

But then begins a journey in my head

To work my mind, when body's work's expired;

For then my thoughts, from far where I abide,

Intend a zealous pilgrimage to thee,

And keep my drooping eyelids open wide,

Looking on darkness which the blind do see;

Save that my soul's imaginary sight

Presents thy shadow to my sightless view,

Which like a jewel, hung in ghastly night,

Makes black night beauteous, and her old face new.

    Lo, thus by day my limbs, by night my mind,

    For thee, and for myself, no quiet find.

28

How can I then return in happy plight

That am debarred the benefit of rest?

When day's oppression is not eased by night,

But day by night and night by day oppressed,[1]

And each, though enemies to either's reign,

Do in consent shake hands to torture me,

The one[2] by toil, the other to complain

How far I toil, still farther off from thee.

I tell the day, to please him, thou art bright,

And dost him grace when clouds do blot the heaven;

So flatter I the swart-complexioned[3] night,

When sparkling stars twire not thou gild'st the even;[4]

    But day doth daily draw my sorrows longer,

    And night doth nightly make grief's length seem stronger.

29

When in disgrace with Fortune and men's eyes
I all alone beweep my outcast state,
And trouble deaf heaven with my bootless¹ cries,
And look upon myself, and curse my fate,
Wishing me like to one more rich in hope,
Featured like him,² like him with friends possessed,
Desiring this man's art and that man's scope,³
With what I most enjoy⁴ contented least;
Yet in these thoughts myself almost despising,
Haply⁵ I think on thee, and then my state⁶—
Like to the lark at break of day arising
From sullen earth—sings hymns at heaven's gate;
    For thy sweet love remembered such wealth brings
    That then I scorn to change my state with kings.

30

When to the sessions¹ of sweet silent thought
I summon up remembrance of things past,
I sigh the lack of many a thing I sought,
And with old woes new wail my dear time's waste;²
Then can I drown an eye, unused to flow,³
For precious friends hid in death's dateless⁴ night,
And weep afresh love's long since cancelled woe,
And moan th'expense⁵ of many a vanished sight.
Then can I grieve at grievances foregone,
And heavily from woe to woe tell o'er⁶
The sad account of fore-bemoaned moan,
Which I new pay as if not paid before;
    But if the while I think on thee, dear friend,
    All losses are restored, and sorrows end.

31

Thy bosom is endearèd with all hearts[1]
Which I, by lacking, have supposèd dead;
And there reigns love, and all love's loving parts,[2]
And all those friends which I thought burièd.
How many a holy and obsequious[3] tear
Hath dear religious love stolen from mine eye,
As interest of the dead, which now appear
But things removed that hidden in thee lie.
Thou art the grave where buried love doth live,
Hung with the trophies[4] of my lovers gone,
Who all their parts of me to thee did give;
That due of many, now is thine alone.

 Their images I loved, I view in thee,
 And thou, all they, hast all the all of me.

32[1]

If thou survive my well-contented day,
When that churl death my bones with dust shall cover,
And shalt by fortune[2] once more re-survey
These poor rude lines of thy deceasèd lover:
Compare them with the bett'ring of the time,[3]
And though they be outstripped by every pen,
Reserve them for my love, not for their rhyme,
Exceeded by the height[4] of happier men.
Oh, then vouchsafe me but this loving thought:
"Had my friend's Muse grown with this growing age,
A dearer birth[5] than this his love had brought,
To march in ranks of better equipage;[6]

 But since he died and poets better prove,
 Theirs for their style I'll read, his for his love."

33[1]

Full many a glorious morning have I seen
Flatter the mountain tops with sovereign eye[2]—
Kissing with golden face the meadows green,
Gilding pale streams with heavenly alchemy[3]—
Anon permit the basest clouds to ride,
With ugly rack[4] on his celestial face,
And from the forlorn world his visage hide,
Stealing unseen to west with this disgrace:
Even so my sun[5] one early morn did shine
With all triumphant splendour on my brow;
But out alack, he was but one hour mine,
The region[6] cloud hath masked him from me now.
    Yet him for this, my love no whit disdaineth:
    Suns of the world may stain, when heaven's sun staineth.

34

Why didst thou promise such a beauteous day,
And make me travel forth without my cloak,
To let base clouds o'ertake me in my way,
Hiding thy brav'ry in their rotten smoke?[1]
'Tis not enough that through the cloud thou break,
To dry the rain on my storm-beaten face,
For no man well of such a salve can speak
That heals the wound, and cures not the disgrace;
Nor can thy shame give physic[2] to my grief;
Though thou repent, yet I have still the loss;
Th'offender's sorrow lends but weak relief
To him that bears the strong offence's cross.[3]
    Ah, but those tears are pearl which thy love sheds,
    And they are rich, and ransom all ill deeds.

35

No more be grieved at that which thou hast done.
Roses have thorns, and silver fountains mud;
Clouds and eclipses stain both moon and sun,
And loathsome canker[1] lives in sweetest bud.
All men make faults, and even I in this,
Authorizing thy trespass with compare,[2]
Myself corrupting, salving thy amiss,
Excusing thy sins more than thy sins are:
For to thy sensual fault I bring in sense;[3]
Thy adverse party is thy advocate,[4]
And 'gainst myself a lawful plea commence:
Such civil war is in my love and hate
    That I an accessory needs must be
    To that sweet thief which sourly robs from me.

36[1]

Let me confess that we two must be twain,[2]
Although our undivided loves are one;
So shall those blots[3] that do with me remain,
Without thy help, by me be borne alone.
In our two loves there is but one respect,[4]
Though in our lives a separable spite;
Which, though it alter not love's sole effect,[5]
Yet doth it steal sweet hours from love's delight.
I may not evermore acknowledge thee,
Lest my bewailed guilt should do thee shame,
Nor thou with public kindness honour me,
Unless thou take that honour from thy name:
    But do not so; I love thee in such sort,
    As thou being mine, mine is thy good report.[6]

37

As a decrepit[1] father takes delight
To see his active child do deeds of youth,
So I, made lame[2] by Fortune's dearest spite,
Take all my comfort of thy worth and truth.
For whether beauty, birth, or wealth, or wit,
Or any of these all, or all, or more,
Entitled in thy parts,[3] do crowned sit,
I make my love engrafted to this store:[4]
So then I am not lame, poor, nor despised,
Whilst that this shadow doth such substance[5] give
That I in thy abundance am sufficed,
And by a part of all thy glory live:
    Look what is best, that best I wish in thee;
    This wish I have, then ten times happy me.

38

How can my Muse want[1] subject to invent
While thou dost breathe, that pour'st into my verse
Thine own sweet argument,[2] too excellent
For every vulgar paper to rehearse?
Oh, give thyself the thanks, if aught in me
Worthy perusal stand against thy sight;
For who's so dumb that cannot write to thee,
When thou thyself dost give invention[3] light?
Be thou the tenth Muse,[4] ten times more in worth
Than those old nine which rhymers invocate;
And he that calls on thee, let him bring forth
Eternal numbers[5] to outlive long date.
    If my slight Muse do please these curious days,
    The pain be mine, but thine shall be the praise.

39

Oh, how thy worth with manners may I sing,
When thou art all the better part of me?
What can mine own praise to mine own self bring,
And what is't but mine own, when I praise thee?
Even for[1] this, let us divided live,
And our dear love lose name of single one,
That by this separation I may give
That due to thee which thou deserv'st alone.
O absence, what a torment wouldst thou prove,
Were it not thy sour leisure gave sweet leave
To entertain the time with thoughts of love,
Which time and thoughts so sweetly dost deceive.[2]
    And that thou teachest how to make one twain,
    By praising him here who doth hence remain.

40[1]

Take all my loves, my love; yea, take them all.
What hast thou then more than thou hadst before?
No love, my love, that thou mayst true love call;
All mine was thine, before thou hadst this more:
Then if for my love thou my love[2] receivest,
I cannot blame thee, for my love thou usest;[3]
But yet be blamed, if thou thyself deceivest
By wilful taste of what thyself refusest.
I do forgive thy robb'ry, gentle thief,
Although thou steal thee all my poverty;
And yet love knows it is a greater grief
To bear love's wrong, than hate's known injury.[4]

    Lascivious grace,[5] in whom all ill well shows,
    Kill me with spites; yet we must not be foes.

41

Those pretty wrongs that liberty¹ commits,
When I am sometime absent from thy heart,
Thy beauty and thy years full well befits;
For still temptation follows where thou art.
Gentle thou art, and therefore to be won;
Beauteous thou art, therefore to be assailed;
And when a woman woos, what woman's son
Will sourly leave her till she² have prevailed?
Ay me, but yet thou mightst my seat³ forbear,
And chide thy beauty and thy straying youth,
Who lead thee in their riot even there
Where thou art forced to break a twofold truth:
    Hers by thy beauty tempting her to thee,
    Thine by thy beauty being false to me.

42

That thou hast her it is not all my grief,
And yet it may be said I loved her dearly;
That she hath thee is of my wailing chief,
A loss in love that touches me more nearly.
Loving offenders, thus I will excuse ye:
Thou dost love her, because thou know'st I love her,
And for my sake even so doth she abuse¹ me,
Suff'ring my friend for my sake to approve² her.
If I lose thee, my loss is my love's gain,
And losing her, my friend hath found that loss;
Both find each other, and I lose both twain,
And both for my sake lay on me this cross.
    But here's the joy: my friend and I are one—
    Sweet flattery—then she loves but me alone.

43[1]

When most I wink,[2] then do mine eyes best see;
For all the day they view things unrespected,[3]
But when I sleep, in dreams they look on thee,
And darkly bright, are bright in dark directed.[4]
Then thou whose shadow shadows doth make bright,[5]
How would thy shadow's form, form happy show
To the clear day with thy much clearer light,
When to unseeing eyes thy shade[6] shines so?
How would, I say, mine eyes be blessèd made
By looking on thee in the living day,
When in dead night thy fair imperfect shade
Through heavy sleep on sightless eyes doth stay?
　　All days are nights to see till I see thee,
　　And nights bright days when dreams do show thee me.

44

If the dull substance[1] of my flesh were thought,
Injurious distance should not stop my way;
For then, despite of space, I would be brought
From limits far remote, where thou dost stay.
No matter then although my foot did stand
Upon the farthest earth removed from thee,
For nimble thought can jump both sea and land
As soon as think the place where he would be.
But ah, thought kills me that I am not thought,
To leap large lengths of miles when thou art gone,
But that so much of earth and water wrought,
I must attend time's leisure[2] with my moan;
　　Receiving nought by elements so slow
　　But heavy tears, badges of either's woe.

45

The other two,[1] slight air, and purging fire,
Are both with thee, wherever I abide:
The first my thought, the other my desire,
These, present-absent,[2] with swift motion slide;
For when these quicker elements are gone
In tender embassy of love to thee,
My life being made of four, with two alone
Sinks down to death, oppressed with melancholy,[3]
Until life's composition[4] be recured
By those swift messengers returned from thee,
Who even but now come back again assured
Of thy fair health, recounting it to me.
    This told, I joy; but then no longer glad,
    I send them back again and straight grow sad.

46[1]

Mine eye and heart are at a mortal war
How to divide the conquest of thy sight;
Mine eye, my heart thy picture's sight would bar,[2]
My heart, mine eye the freedom of that right;
My heart doth plead that thou in him dost lie,
A closet never pierced with crystal eyes;
But the defendant[3] doth that plea deny,
And says in him thy fair appearance lies.
To 'cide[4] this title is empanelled
A quest of thoughts, all tenants to the heart,
And by their verdict is determined
The clear eyes' moiety,[5] and the dear heart's part.
    As thus, mine eyes' due is thy outward part,
    And my heart's right, thy inward love of heart.

47

Betwixt mine eye and heart a league[1] is took,
And each doth good turns now unto the other;
When that mine eye is famished for a look,
Or heart in love with sighs himself doth smother,
With my love's picture then my eye doth feast,
And to the painted banquet bids my heart;
Another time mine eye is my heart's guest,
And in his thoughts of love doth share a part.
So either by thy picture or my love,
Thyself away, art present still with me;
For thou no further than my thoughts canst move,
And I am still with them,[2] and they with thee;
    Or if they sleep, thy picture in my sight
    Awakes my heart to heart's and eye's delight.

48

How careful was I, when I took my way,
Each trifle under truest[1] bars to thrust,
That to my use it might unused stay
From hands of falsehood, in sure wards[2] of trust;
But thou, to whom my jewels trifles are,
Most worthy comfort, now my greatest grief,
Thou best of dearest, and mine only care,
Art left the prey of every vulgar thief.
Thee have I not locked up in any chest,
Save where thou art not, though I feel thou art,
Within the gentle closure of my breast,
From whence at pleasure thou mayst come and part;[3]
    And even thence thou wilt be stol'n, I fear,
    For truth proves thievish for a prize so dear.

49

Against[1] that time, if ever that time come,
When I shall see thee frown on my defects;
Whenas thy love hath cast his utmost sum,[2]
Called to that audit by advised respects;[3]
Against that time when thou shalt strangely pass,
And scarcely greet me with that sun, thine eye,
When love, converted from the thing it was,
Shall reasons find of settled gravity;[4]
Against that time do I ensconce[5] me here,
Within the knowledge of mine own desert,[6]
And this my hand against myself uprear,
To guard the lawful reasons on thy part.
    To leave poor me, thou hast the strength of laws,
    Since why to love, I can allege no cause.

50[1]

How heavy[2] do I journey on the way
When what I seek, my weary travel's end,
Doth teach that ease and that repose to say,
"Thus far the miles are measured from thy friend."
The beast that bears me, tired with my woe,
Plods dully on to bear that weight in me,
As if by some instinct the wretch did know
His rider loved not speed being made from thee.
The bloody spur cannot provoke him on
That sometimes anger thrusts into his hide,
Which heavily he answers with a groan,
More sharp to me than spurring to his side,
    For that same groan doth put this in my mind:
    My grief lies onward and my joy behind.

51

Thus can my love excuse the slow offence
Of my dull bearer, when from thee I speed:
From where thou art, why should I haste me thence?
Till I return, of posting[1] is no need.
Oh, what excuse will my poor beast then find,
When swift extremity[2] can seem but slow?
Then should I spur, though mounted on the wind;
In winged speed no motion shall I know;
Then can no horse with my desire keep pace;
Therefore desire, of perfect'st love being made,
Shall weigh[3] no dull flesh in his fiery race,
But love, for love, thus shall excuse my jade:[4]
    Since from thee going he went wilful-slow,
    Towards thee I'll run, and give him leave to go.

52

So am I as the rich, whose blessèd key
Can bring him to his sweet up-lockèd treasure,
The which he will not every hour survey,
For[1] blunting the fine point of seldom pleasure;
Therefore are feasts so solemn and so rare,
Since, seldom coming, in the long year set,
Like stones of worth they thinly placèd are,
Or captain jewels in the carcanet.[2]
So is the time that keeps you[3] as my chest,
Or as the wardrobe which the robe doth hide,
To make some special instant special blessed
By new unfolding his imprisoned pride.
    Blessed are you, whose worthiness gives scope,
      Being had, to triumph; being lacked, to hope.

53

What is your substance, whereof are you made,
That millions of strange shadows[1] on you tend?
Since every one hath every one one shade,[2]
And you, but one, can every shadow lend;
Describe Adonis,[3] and the counterfeit
Is poorly imitated after you;
On Helen's[4] cheek all art of beauty set
And you in Grecian tires are painted new;
Speak of the spring, and foison[5] of the year:
The one doth shadow of your beauty show,
The other as your bounty doth appear,
And you in every blessed shape we know.
    In all external grace you have some part,
      But you like none, none you, for constant heart.

54

Oh, how much more doth beauty beauteous seem
By that sweet ornament which truth doth give!
The rose looks fair, but fairer we it deem
For that sweet odour which doth in it live;
The canker blooms[1] have full as deep a dye
As the perfumèd tincture of the roses,
Hang on such thorns, and play as wantonly,
When summer's breath their maskèd buds discloses;
But, for their virtue only is their show,
They live unwooed, and unrespected[2] fade,
Die to themselves. Sweet roses do not so;
Of their sweet deaths are sweetest odours made:[3]
    And so of you, beauteous and lovely youth,
      When that shall vade,[4] my[5] verse distils your truth.

55

Not marble, nor the gilded monuments
Of princes, shall outlive this powerful rhyme;
But you shall shine more bright in these contents
Than unswept stone,[1] besmeared with sluttish time.
When wasteful war shall statues overturn,
And broils[2] root out the work of masonry,
Nor Mars[3] his sword, nor war's quick fire, shall burn
The living record of your memory.
'Gainst death, and all-oblivious enmity[4]
Shall you pace forth; your praise shall still find room
Even in the eyes of all posterity
That wear this world out to the ending doom.
    So till the judgement that yourself arise,
      You live in this, and dwell in lovers' eyes.

56

Sweet love, renew thy force; be it not said
Thy edge should blunter be than appetite,[1]
Which but today by feeding is allayed,
Tomorrow sharpened in his former might.
So, love, be thou; although today thou fill
Thy hungry eyes, even till they wink with fullness,[2]
Tomorrow see again, and do not kill
The spirit of love with a perpetual dullness;
Let this sad interim like the ocean be
Which parts the shore, where two contracted new[3]
Come daily to the banks, that when they see
Return of love, more blessed may be the view;
    Or call it winter, which being full of care
    Makes summer's welcome thrice more wished, more rare.

57[1]

Being your slave, what should I do but tend[2]
Upon the hours and times of your desire?
I have no precious time at all to spend,
Nor services to do, till you require;
Nor dare I chide the world-without-end[3] hour
Whilst I, my sovereign, watch the clock for you,
Nor think the bitterness of absence sour
When you have bid your servant once adieu;
Nor dare I question with my jealous thought
Where you may be, or your affairs suppose,
But like a sad slave stay and think of naught,
Save, where you are, how happy you make those.
    So true a fool is love, that in your will,[4]
    Though you do anything, he thinks no ill.

58

That god forbid, that made me first your slave,
I should in thought control[1] your times of pleasure,
Or at your hand th'account of hours to crave,
Being your vassal bound to stay[2] your leisure.
Oh, let me suffer, being at your beck,
Th'imprisoned absence of your liberty,[3]
And patience-tame to sufferance bide each check,[4]
Without accusing you of injury.
Be where you list,[5] your charter[6] is so strong
That you yourself may privilege your time
To what you will; to you it doth belong
Yourself to pardon of self-doing crime.
    I am to wait, though waiting so be hell,
      Not blame your pleasure be it ill or well.

59

If there be nothing new, but that which is
Hath been before, how are our brains beguiled,[1]
Which, labouring for invention,[2] bear amiss
The second burden of a former child?
Oh, that record[3] could with a backward look,
Even of five hundred courses of the sun,
Show me your image in some antique book,
Since mind at first in character was done,[4]
That I might see what the old world could say
To this composèd wonder of your frame;
Whether we are mended,[5] or whe'er better they,
Or whether revolution[6] be the same.
    Oh, sure I am, the wits of former days
      To subjects worse have given admiring praise.

60

Like as the waves make towards the pebbled shore,
So do our minutes hasten to their end,
Each changing place with that which goes before,
In sequent toil all forwards do contend.[1]
Nativity,[2] once in the main of light,
Crawls to maturity; wherewith, being crowned,
Crooked eclipses 'gainst his glory fight,[3]
And Time that gave, doth now his gift confound.
Time doth transfix[4] the flourish set on youth,
And delves the parallels[5] in beauty's brow;
Feeds on the rarities of nature's truth,
And nothing stands but for his scythe to mow.
    And yet to times in hope my verse shall stand,
    Praising thy worth, despite his cruel hand.

61

Is it thy will thy image should keep open
My heavy eyelids to the weary night?
Dost thou desire my slumbers should be broken,
While shadows like to thee do mock my sight?
Is it thy spirit that thou send'st from thee
So far from home into my deeds to pry,
To find out shames and idle hours in me,
The scope and tenor[1] of thy jealousy?
Oh, no, thy love, though much, is not so great;
It is my love that keeps mine eye awake,
Mine own true love that doth my rest defeat,
To play the watchman ever for thy sake.
    For thee watch I, whilst thou dost wake elsewhere,
    From me far off, with others all too near.

62

Sin of self-love possesseth all mine eye,

And all my soul, and all my every part;

And for this sin there is no remedy,

It is so grounded inward in my heart.

Methinks no face so gracious is as mine,

No shape so true, no truth of such account,

And for myself mine own worth do define,

As I all other in all worths surmount.

But when my glass shows me myself indeed,

Beated[1] and chapped with tanned antiquity,[2]

Mine own self-love quite contrary I read;

Self, so self-loving, were iniquity.

    'Tis thee—my self—that for myself I praise,

    Painting my age with beauty of thy days.

63

Against[1] my love shall be as I am now,

With Time's injurious hand crushed and o'erworn;

When hours have drained his blood, and filled his brow

With lines and wrinkles; when his youthful morn

Hath travelled[2] on to age's steepy[3] night,

And all those beauties whereof now he's king

Are vanishing, or vanished out of sight,

Stealing away the treasure of his spring;

For such a time do I now fortify

Against confounding age's cruel knife,

That he shall never cut from memory

My sweet love's beauty, though my lover's life.

    His beauty shall in these black lines be seen,

    And they shall live, and he in them still green.

64[1]

When I have seen by Time's fell[2] hand defaced
The rich proud cost[3] of outworn buried age;
When sometime lofty towers I see down-razed,
And brass eternal[4] slave to mortal rage;
When I have seen the hungry ocean gain
Advantage on the kingdom of the shore,
And the firm soil win of the wat'ry main,[5]
Increasing store with loss,[6] and loss with store;
When I have seen such interchange of state,
Or state itself confounded to decay,
Ruin hath taught me thus to ruminate
That Time will come and take my love away.
    This thought is as a death, which cannot choose
    But weep to have that which it fears to lose.

65

Since brass, nor stone, nor earth, nor boundless sea,[1]
But sad mortality[2] o'ersways their power,
How with this rage shall beauty hold a plea,
Whose action is no stronger than a flower?
Oh, how shall summer's honey breath hold out
Against the wrackful siege of batt'ring days[3]
When rocks impregnable are not so stout,
Nor gates of steel so strong, but time decays?
Oh, fearful meditation! Where, alack,
Shall Time's best jewel from Time's chest lie hid?[4]
Or what strong hand can hold his swift foot back,
Or who his spoil of beauty can forbid?
    O, none, unless this miracle have might,
    That in black ink my love may still shine bright.

66

Tired with all these[1] for restful death I cry:
As to behold desert[2] a beggar born,
And needy nothing[3] trimmed in jollity,
And purest faith unhappily forsworn,[4]
And gilded honour shamefully misplaced,
And maiden virtue rudely strumpeted,
And right perfection wrongfully disgraced,
And strength by limping sway[5] disabled,
And art made tongue-tied by authority,
And folly, doctor-like,[6] controlling skill,
And simple truth miscalled simplicity,[7]
And captive good attending captain ill:[8]
    Tired with all these, from these would I be gone,
    Save that to die I leave my love alone.

67[1]

Ah, wherefore[2] with infection[3] should he live,
And with his presence grace impiety,
That sin by him advantage should achieve,[4]
And lace[5] itself with his society?
Why should false painting imitate his cheek,
And steal dead seeming of his living hue?
Why should poor beauty indirectly seek
Roses of shadow,[6] since his rose is true?
Why should he live, now nature bankrupt is,
Beggared of blood to blush through lively veins?
For she hath no exchequer[7] now but his,
And proud of many, lives upon his gains.
    O, him she stores,[8] to show what wealth she had
    In days long since, before these last so bad.[9]

68

Thus is his cheek the map of days outworn,
When beauty lived and died as flowers do now,
Before these bastard signs of fair[1] were born,
Or durst inhabit on a living brow;
Before the golden tresses of the dead,[2]
The right of sepulchres,[3] were shorn away,
To live a second life on second head;
Ere beauty's dead fleece made another gay.
In him those holy antique hours[4] are seen,
Without all ornament, itself and true,
Making no summer of another's green,
Robbing no old to dress his beauty new;
    And him as for a map doth Nature store,
    To show false Art what beauty was of yore.

69

Those parts of thee that the world's eye doth view
Want[1] nothing that the thought of hearts can mend;
All tongues, the voice of souls, give thee that due,
Utt'ring bare truth, even so as foes commend;[2]
Thy outward[3] thus with outward praise is crowned.
But those same tongues that give thee so thine own
In other accents do this praise confound,[4]
By seeing farther than the eye hath shown;
They look into the beauty of thy mind,
And that in guess they measure by thy deeds;[5]
Then, churls, their thoughts, although their eyes were kind,
To thy fair flower add the rank smell of weeds.
    But why thy odour matcheth not thy show,
    The soil[6] is this, that thou dost common[7] grow.

70

That thou art blamed shall not be thy defect,
For slander's mark was ever yet the fair;[1]
The ornament of beauty is suspect,
A crow that flies in heaven's sweetest air.
So thou be good, slander doth but approve
Thy worth the greater, being wooed of time;[2]
For canker vice[3] the sweetest buds doth love,
And thou present'st a pure unstainèd prime.[4]
Thou hast passed by the ambush of young days,[5]
Either not assailed, or victor, being charged;
Yet this thy praise cannot be so thy praise,
To tie up envy, evermore enlarged.
    If some suspect of ill[6] masked not thy show,
    Then thou alone kingdoms of hearts shouldst owe.[7]

71[1]

No longer mourn for me when I am dead
Than you shall hear the surly sullen bell[2]
Give warning to the world that I am fled
From this vile world, with vilest worms to dwell.
Nay, if you read this line, remember not
The hand that writ it, for I love you so
That I in your sweet thoughts would be forgot,
If thinking on me then should make you woe.
Oh, if, I say, you look upon this verse,
When I perhaps compounded am with clay,[3]
Do not so much as my poor name rehearse,[4]
But let your love even with my life decay,
    Lest the wise world should look into your moan,
    And mock you with me after I am gone.

72

O, lest the world should task[1] you to recite
What merit lived in me that you should love,
After my death, dear love, forget me quite,
For you in me can nothing worthy prove—
Unless you would devise some virtuous lie
To do more for me than mine own desert,
And hang more praise upon deceasèd I
Than niggard truth would willingly impart.
O, lest your true love may seem false in this,
That you for love speak well of me untrue,[2]
My name be buried where my body is,
And live no more to shame nor me, nor you.
    For I am shamed by that which I bring forth,[3]
    And so should you, to love things nothing worth.

73[1]

That time of year thou mayst in me behold,
When yellow leaves, or none, or few do hang
Upon those boughs which shake against the cold,
Bare ruined choirs where late[2] the sweet birds sang.[3]
In me thou seest the twilight of such day
As after sunset fadeth in the west,
Which by and by black night doth take away,
Death's second self, that seals[4] up all in rest.
In me thou seest the glowing of such fire
That on the ashes of his youth doth lie,
As the deathbed, whereon it must expire,[5]
Consumed with that which it was nourished by.
    This thou perceiv'st, which makes thy love more strong,
    To love that well, which thou must leave ere long.

74

But be contented when that fell[1] arrest
Without all bail shall carry me away;
My life hath in this line[2] some interest,
Which for memorial still[3] with thee shall stay.
When thou reviewest this, thou dost review
The very part was consecrate to thee;
The earth can have but earth, which is his[4] due,
My spirit is thine, the better part of me;
So then thou hast but lost the dregs of life,
The prey of worms, my body being dead,
The coward conquest of a wretch's knife,
Too base of thee to be remembered.
    The worth of that, is that which it contains,
    And that is this, and this with thee remains.

75

So are you to my thoughts as food to life,[1]
Or as sweet-seasoned showers are to the ground;
And for the peace of you[2] I hold such strife
As 'twixt a miser and his wealth is found.
Now proud as an enjoyer, and anon
Doubting the filching age will steal his treasure;
Now counting[3] best to be with you alone,
Then bettered[4] that the world may see my pleasure;
Sometime all full with feasting on your sight,
And by and by clean starvèd for a look,
Possessing or pursuing no delight
Save what is had, or must from you be took.
    Thus do I pine and surfeit day by day,
    Or gluttoning on all, or all away.[5]

76

Why is my verse so barren of new pride?[1]
So far from variation or quick change?
Why with the time do I not glance aside
To new-found methods and to compounds strange?[2]
Why write I still all one, ever the same,
And keep invention in a noted weed,[3]
That every word doth almost tell my name,
Showing their birth, and where they did proceed?
Oh, know, sweet love, I always write of you,
And you and love are still[4] my argument:
So all my best is dressing old words new,
Spending again what is already spent:
    For as the sun is daily new and old,
    So is my love still telling what is told.

77

Thy glass[1] will show thee how thy beauties wear,
Thy dial how thy precious minutes waste,
The vacant leaves[2] thy mind's imprint will bear,
And of this book, this learning mayst thou taste.
The wrinkles which thy glass will truly show
Of mouthèd graves will give thee memory;
Thou by thy dial's shady stealth mayst know
Time's thievish progress to eternity.
Look what thy memory cannot contain,
Commit to these waste blanks, and thou shalt find
Those children[3] nursed, delivered from thy brain,
To take a new acquaintance of thy mind.
    These offices,[4] so oft as thou wilt look,
    Shall profit thee, and much enrich thy book.

78[1]

So oft have I invoked thee for my Muse,
And found such fair assistance in my verse,
As every alien pen hath got my use,[2]
And under thee their poesy disperse.[3]
Thine eyes, that taught the dumb on high to sing,
And heavy ignorance aloft to fly,
Have added feathers to the learnèd's wing,
And given grace[4] a double majesty.
Yet be most proud of that which I compile,[5]
Whose influence is thine, and born of thee;
In others' works thou dost but mend the style,
And arts with thy sweet graces gracèd be.
    But thou art all my art, and dost advance,
    As high as learning, my rude ignorance.

79

Whilst I alone did call upon thy aid
My verse alone had all thy gentle grace;
But now my gracious numbers[1] are decayed,
And my sick Muse doth give another place.[2]
I grant, sweet love, thy lovely argument[3]
Deserves the travail of a worthier pen;
Yet what of thee thy poet doth invent
He robs thee of, and pays it thee again;
He lends thee virtue, and he stole that word
From thy behaviour; beauty doth he give,
And found it in thy cheek; he can afford
No praise to thee, but what in thee doth live.
    Then thank him not for that which he doth say,
    Since what he owes thee, thou thyself dost pay.

80

Oh, how I faint when I of you do write,
Knowing a better spirit[1] doth use your name,
And in the praise thereof spends all his might,
To make me tongue-tied speaking of your fame.
But since your worth, wide as the ocean is,
The humble as the proudest sail doth bear,
My saucy bark,[2] inferior far to his,
On your broad main[3] doth wilfully appear.
Your shallowest help will hold me up afloat,
Whilst he upon your soundless[4] deep doth ride;
Or, being wrecked, I am a worthless boat,
He of tall building,[5] and of goodly pride.
    Then if he thrive, and I be cast away,
    The worst was this: my love was my decay.

81

Or[1] I shall live, your epitaph to make,
Or you survive when I in earth am rotten;
From hence[2] your memory death cannot take,
Although in me each part will be forgotten.
Your name from hence immortal life shall have,
Though I, once gone, to all the world must die;
The earth can yield me but a common grave,
When you entombèd in men's eyes shall lie.
Your monument shall be my gentle verse,
Which eyes not yet created shall o'er-read,
And tongues-to-be your being shall rehearse,
When all the breathers of this world are dead.
    You still shall live, such virtue[3] hath my pen,
      Where breath most breathes, even in the mouths of men.

82[1]

I grant thou wert not married to my Muse,
And therefore mayst without attaint[2] o'erlook
The dedicated words[3] which writers use
Of their fair subject, blessing every book.
Thou art as fair in knowledge as in hue,
Finding thy worth a limit past my praise,[4]
And therefore art enforced to seek anew
Some fresher stamp of the time-bettering days.[5]
And do so, love; yet when they have devised
What strainèd touches rhetoric can lend,
Thou, truly fair, wert truly sympathized[6]
In true plain words, by thy true-telling friend;
    And their gross painting[7] might be better used
    Where cheeks need blood; in thee it is abused.

83

I never saw that you did painting need,
And therefore to your fair[1] no painting set;
I found (or thought I found) you did exceed
The barren tender[2] of a poet's debt;
And therefore have I slept in your report,
That you yourself, being extant,[3] well might show
How far a modern quill doth come too short,
Speaking of worth, what worth in you doth grow.
This silence for my sin you did impute,
Which shall be most my glory, being dumb;
For I impair not beauty, being mute,
When others would give life, and bring a tomb.[4]
    There lives more life in one of your fair eyes
    Than both your poets can in praise devise.

84

Who is it that says most which can say more[1]
Than this rich praise: that you alone are you?
In whose confine immured is the store[2]
Which should example where your equal grew?
Lean penury[3] within that pen doth dwell
That to his subject lends not some small glory;
But he that writes of you, if he can tell
That you are you, so dignifies his story.
Let him but copy what in you is writ,
Not making worse what nature made so clear,
And such a counterpart shall fame his wit,[4]
Making his style admired everywhere.
    You to your beauteous blessings add a curse,
    Being fond on[5] praise, which makes your praises worse.

85

My tongue-tied Muse in manners holds her still,
While comments of your praise richly compiled
Reserve thy character[1] with golden quill,
And precious phrase by all the Muses filed.[2]
I think good thoughts, whilst other write good words,
And like unlettered[3] clerk still cry "Amen"
To every hymn that able spirit affords
In polished form of well refinèd pen.
Hearing you praised, I say "'Tis so, 'tis true",
And to the most of praise[4] add something more;
But that is in my thought, whose love to you,
Though words come hindmost, holds his[5] rank before;
    Then others for the breath of words respect,
    Me for my dumb thoughts, speaking in effect.

86

Was it the proud full sail of his[1] great verse,
Bound for the prize[2] of all-too-precious you,
That did my ripe thoughts in my brain inhearse,[3]
Making their tomb the womb wherein they grew?
Was it his spirit, by spirits taught to write
Above a mortal pitch, that struck me dead?
No, neither he, nor his compeers by night[4]
Giving him aid, my verse astonishèd.
He, nor that affable familiar ghost
Which nightly gulls him with intelligence,[5]
As victors of my silence cannot boast;
I was not sick of any fear from thence.
    But when your countenance filled up his line,[6]
    Then lacked I matter, that enfeebled mine.

87

Farewell! thou art too dear for my possessing,
And like enough thou know'st thy estimate;[1]
The charter[2] of thy worth gives thee releasing;
My bonds in thee are all determinate.[3]
For how do I hold thee but by thy granting,
And for that riches where is my deserving?
The cause of this fair gift in me is wanting,[4]
And so my patent[5] back again is swerving.
Thyself thou gav'st, thy own worth then not knowing,
Or me, to whom thou gav'st it, else mistaking;
So thy great gift upon misprision[6] growing
Comes home again, on better judgement making.
  Thus have I had thee as a dream doth flatter,
  In sleep a king, but waking no such matter.

88

When thou shalt be disposed to set me light[1]
And place my merit in the eye of scorn,
Upon thy side against myself I'll fight,
And prove thee virtuous, though thou art forsworn.
With mine own weakness being best acquainted,
Upon thy part[2] I can set down a story
Of faults concealed, wherein I am attainted,[3]
That thou, in losing me, shall win much glory;
And I by this will be a gainer too,
For bending all my loving thoughts on thee,
The injuries that to myself I do,
Doing thee vantage, double-vantage me.
  Such is my love, to thee I so belong,
  That for thy right myself will bear all wrong.

89[1]

Say that thou didst forsake me for some fault,
And I will comment upon that offence;
Speak of my lameness, and I straight will halt,[2]
Against thy reasons making no defence.
Thou canst not, love, disgrace me half so ill,
To set a form upon desired change,[3]
As I'll myself disgrace, knowing thy will;
I will acquaintance strangle and look strange,[4]
Be absent from thy walks, and in my tongue
Thy sweet beloved name no more shall dwell,
Lest I, too much profane, should do it wrong,
And haply[5] of our old acquaintance tell.
    For thee, against myself I'll vow debate,
    For I must ne'er love him whom thou dost hate.

90

Then hate me when thou wilt, if ever, now,
Now, while the world is bent my deeds to cross,
Join with the spite of fortune, make me bow,
And do not drop in for an after-loss.[1]
Ah, do not, when my heart hath 'scaped this sorrow,
Come in the rearward of a conquered woe;[2]
Give not a windy night a rainy morrow,
To linger out[3] a purposed overthrow.
If thou wilt leave me, do not leave me last,
When other petty griefs have done their spite;
But in the onset come, so shall I taste
At first the very worst of fortune's might;
    And other strains of woe, which now seem woe,
    Compared with loss of thee, will not seem so.

91

Some glory in their birth, some in their skill,
Some in their wealth, some in their body's force,
Some in their garments, though new-fangled ill,[1]
Some in their hawks and hounds, some in their horse;
And every humour hath his adjunct pleasure,
Wherein it finds a joy above the rest.
But these particulars are not my measure;
All these I better in one general best.
Thy love is better than high birth to me,
Richer than wealth, prouder than garments' cost,
Of more delight than hawks or horses be;
And having thee, of all men's pride I boast—
　　Wretched in this alone, that thou mayst take
　　All this away, and me most wretched make.

92[1]

But do thy worst to steal thyself away,
For term of life thou art assurèd mine,
And life no longer than thy love will stay,
For it depends upon that love of thine.
Then need I not to fear the worst of wrongs,
When in the least of them[2] my life hath end;
I see a better state to me belongs
Than that which on thy humour[3] doth depend.
Thou canst not vex me with inconstant mind,
Since that my life on thy revolt doth lie.[4]
Oh, what a happy title do I find,
Happy to have thy love, happy to die!
 But what's so blessed-fair that fears no blot?
 Thou mayst be false, and yet I know it not.

93

So shall I live, supposing[1] thou art true,
Like a deceived husband; so love's face
May still seem love to me, though altered new,
Thy looks with me, thy heart in other place.[2]
For there can live no hatred in thine eye,
Therefore in that I cannot know thy change.
In many's looks, the false heart's history
Is writ in moods and frowns and wrinkles strange.
But heaven in thy creation did decree
That in thy face sweet love should ever dwell;
Whate'er thy thoughts or thy heart's workings be,
Thy looks should nothing thence but sweetness tell.
 How like Eve's apple doth thy beauty grow,
 If thy sweet virtue answer not thy show.

94[1]

They that have power to hurt, and will do none,
That do not do the thing they most do show,[2]
Who, moving others, are themselves as stone,
Unmoved, cold, and to temptation slow:
They rightly do inherit heaven's graces,
And husband[3] nature's riches from expense;
They are the lords and owners of their faces,
Others, but stewards[4] of their excellence.
The summer's flower is to the summer sweet,
Though to itself it only live and die,
But if that flower with base infection meet,
The basest weed outbraves his dignity:
    For sweetest things turn sourest by their deeds;
    Lilies that fester smell far worse than weeds.

95

How sweet and lovely dost thou make the shame
Which, like a canker in the fragrant rose,
Doth spot the beauty of thy budding name!
Oh, in what sweets dost thou thy sins enclose!
That tongue that tells the story of thy days,
Making lascivious comments on thy sport,[1]
Cannot dispraise; but in a kind of praise,
Naming thy name, blesses an ill report.
Oh, what a mansion have those vices got,
Which for their habitation chose out thee,
Where beauty's veil doth cover every blot,
And all things turns to fair that eyes can see!
    Take heed, dear heart, of this large[2] privilege;
    The hardest knife ill-used doth lose his edge.

96

Some say thy fault is youth, some wantonness;[1]
Some say thy grace is youth and gentle sport;[2]
Both grace and faults are loved of more and less;[3]
Thou mak'st faults graces, that to thee resort:
As on the finger of a thronèd queen
The basest jewel will be well esteemed,
So are those errors that in thee are seen
To truths translated, and for true things deemed.
How many lambs might the stern wolf betray
If like a lamb he could his looks translate![4]
How many gazers mightst thou lead away
If thou wouldst use the strength of all thy state!
 But do not so; I love thee in such sort,
 As, thou being mine, mine is thy good report.[5]

97

How like a winter hath my absence been
From thee, the pleasure of the fleeting year![1]
What freezings have I felt, what dark days seen,
What old December's bareness everywhere!
And yet this time removed was summer's time,
The teeming[2] autumn big with rich increase
Bearing the wanton burden of the prime,[3]
Like widowed wombs after their lords' decease:
Yet this abundant issue[4] seemed to me
But hope of orphans, and unfathered fruit;
For summer and his pleasures wait on thee,
And thou away, the very birds are mute;
 Or if they sing, 'tis with so dull a cheer[5]
 That leaves look pale, dreading the winter's near.

98

From you have I been absent in the spring,
When proud-pied¹ April, dressed in all his trim,
Hath put a spirit of youth in every thing,
That heavy Saturn² laughed and leaped with him.
Yet nor the lays³ of birds, nor the sweet smell
Of different flowers in odour and in hue,
Could make me any summer's story tell,
Or from their proud lap pluck them where they grew;
Nor⁴ did I wonder at the lily's white,
Nor praise the deep vermilion in the rose;
They were but sweet, but figures⁵ of delight
Drawn after you, you pattern of all those.
    Yet seemed it winter still, and, you away,
    As with your shadow⁶ I with these did play.

99¹

The forward² violet thus did I chide:
"Sweet thief, whence didst thou steal thy sweet that smells,
If not from my love's breath? The purple pride
Which on thy soft cheek for complexion dwells
In my love's veins thou hast too grossly³ dyed."
The lily I condemnèd for thy hand,
And buds of marjoram had stol'n thy hair;
The roses fearfully on thorns did stand,
One blushing shame, another white despair;
A third, nor⁴ red, nor white, had stol'n of both,
And to his robbery had annexed thy breath;
But for his theft, in pride of all his growth
A vengeful canker⁵ ate him up to death.⁶
    More flowers I noted, yet I none could see,
    But sweet, or colour, it had stol'n from thee.

100

Where art thou, Muse, that thou forget'st so long
To speak of that which gives thee all thy might?
Spend'st thou thy fury¹ on some worthless song,
Darkening² thy power to lend base subjects light?
Return, forgetful Muse, and straight redeem,
In gentle numbers,³ time so idly spent;
Sing to the ear that doth thy lays⁴ esteem,
And gives thy pen both skill and argument.⁵
Rise, resty⁶ Muse; my love's sweet face survey,
If time have any wrinkle graven there;
If any, be a satire to decay,⁷
And make time's spoils despised everywhere.
    Give my love fame faster than time wastes life,
    So thou prevent'st his scythe and crooked knife.

101

O truant Muse, what shall be thy amends
For thy neglect of truth in beauty dyed?¹
Both truth and beauty on my love depends;
So dost thou too, and therein dignified.
Make answer, Muse, wilt thou not haply say,
"Truth needs no colour² with his colour fixed,
Beauty no pencil, beauty's truth to lay,³
But best is best if never intermixed"?
Because he needs no praise, wilt thou be dumb?
Excuse not silence so, for't lies in thee
To make him much outlive a gilded tomb,
And to be praised of ages yet to be.
    Then do thy office, Muse; I teach thee how
    To make him seem long hence, as he shows now.⁴

102

My love is strengthened, though more weak in seeming;
I love not less, though less the show appear.
That love is merchandised,¹ whose rich esteeming²
The owner's tongue doth publish everywhere.
Our love was new, and then but in the spring,
When I was wont to³ greet it with my lays,⁴
As Philomel⁵ in summer's front⁶ doth sing,
And stops her pipe in growth of riper days.
Not that the summer is less pleasant now
Than when her mournful hymns did hush the night;
But that wild music burdens⁷ every bough,
And sweets grown common lose their dear delight.
   Therefore, like her, I sometime hold my tongue,
   Because I would not dull you with my song.

103

Alack, what poverty¹ my Muse brings forth,
That, having such a scope to show her pride,
The argument all bare² is of more worth
Than when it hath my added praise beside.
O blame me not if I no more can write!
Look in your glass,³ and there appears a face
That over-goes my blunt invention quite,
Dulling my lines, and doing me disgrace.
Were it not sinful, then, striving to mend,
To mar the subject that before was well?
For to no other pass⁴ my verses tend
Than of your graces and your gifts to tell.
   And more, much more, than in my verse can sit
   Your own glass shows you, when you look in it.

104[1]

To me, fair friend, you never can be old;
For as you were when first your eye I eyed,
Such seems your beauty still: three winters cold
Have from the forests shook three summers' pride;
Three beauteous springs to yellow autumn turned
In process of the seasons have I seen;
Three April perfumes in three hot Junes burned,
Since first I saw you fresh, which yet are green.
Ah, yet doth beauty, like a dial hand,
Steal from his figure, and no pace perceived;[2]
So your sweet hue, which methinks still doth stand,[3]
Hath motion, and mine eye may be deceived;
    For fear of which, hear this, thou age unbred,
    Ere you were born was beauty's summer dead.

105

Let not my love be called idolatry,
Nor my beloved as an idol show,[1]
Since all alike my songs and praises be
To one, of one, still such, and ever so.[2]
Kind is my love today, tomorrow kind,
Still constant in a wondrous excellence;
Therefore my verse, to constancy confined,
One thing expressing, leaves out difference.
Fair, kind, and true is all my argument;
Fair, kind, and true, varying to other words,
And in this change[3] is my invention spent,
Three themes in one, which wondrous scope affords.
    Fair, kind, and true have often lived alone,
    Which three, till now, never kept seat in one.[4]

106

When in the chronicle of wasted[1] time
I see descriptions of the fairest wights,[2]
And beauty making beautiful old rhyme,
In praise of ladies dead, and lovely knights;
Then in the blazon[3] of sweet beauty's best,
Of hand, of foot, of lip, of eye, of brow,
I see their antique[4] pen would have expressed
Even such a beauty as you master now.
So all their praises are but prophecies
Of this our time, all you prefiguring;
And for they looked but with divining[5] eyes
They had not skill enough your worth to sing.
    For we which now behold these present days
    Have eyes to wonder, but lack tongues to praise.

107

Not mine own fears, nor the prophetic soul
Of the wide world, dreaming on things to come,[1]
Can yet the lease[2] of my true love control,
Supposed as forfeit to a confinèd doom.[3]
The mortal moon hath her eclipse endured,[4]
And the sad augurs mock their own presage;[5]
Incertainties now crown themselves assured,
And peace proclaims olives of endless age.[6]
Now with the drops of this most balmy[7] time
My love looks fresh, and death to me subscribes,[8]
Since, spite of him, I'll live in this poor rhyme,
While he insults o'er dull and speechless tribes;
    And thou in this shalt find thy monument,
    When tyrants' crests and tombs of brass are spent.[9]

108

What's in the brain that ink may character[1]
Which hath not figured[2] to thee my true spirit?
What's new to speak, what now to register,
That may express my love, or thy dear merit?
Nothing, sweet boy; but yet, like prayers divine,
I must each day say o'er the very same,
Counting no old thing old;[3] thou mine, I thine,
Even as when first I hallowed thy fair name.
So that eternal love, in love's fresh case,
Weighs not the dust and injury of age,
Nor gives to necessary wrinkles place
But makes antiquity for aye his page,[4]
    Finding the first conceit[5] of love there bred,
      Where time and outward form would show it dead.

109[1]

O never say that I was false of heart,
Though absence seemed my flame to qualify;[2]
As easy might I from myself depart
As from my soul which in thy breast doth lie:
That is my home of love; if I have ranged,[3]
Like him that travels I return again,
Just to the time,[4] not with the time exchanged,
So that myself bring water for my stain;[5]
Never believe, though in my nature reigned
All frailties that besiege all kinds of blood,[6]
That it could so preposterously be stained,
To leave for nothing all thy sum of good:
    For nothing this wide universe I call,
      Save thou, my rose; in it thou art my all.

110[1]

Alas, 'tis true, I have gone here and there,
And made myself a motley[2] to the view,
Gored[3] mine own thoughts, sold cheap what is most dear,
Made old offences of affections new.[4]
Most true it is that I have looked on truth
Askance and strangely; but by all above,
These blenches[5] gave my heart another youth,
And worse essays[6] proved thee my best of love.
Now all is done, save what shall have no end;
Mine appetite I never more will grind
On newer proof, to try an older friend,
A god in love, to whom I am confined.
　　Then give me welcome, next my heaven the best,
　　Even to thy pure and most most loving breast.

111

Oh, for my sake do you with Fortune chide,
The guilty goddess of my harmful deeds,
That[1] did not better for my life provide
Than public means, which public manners breeds.[2]
Thence comes it that my name receives a brand,[3]
And almost thence my nature is subdued
To what it works in, like the dyer's hand;[4]
Pity me then, and wish I were renewed,
Whilst like a willing patient I will drink
Potions of eisel[5] 'gainst my strong infection;[6]
No bitterness that I will bitter think,
Nor double penance to correct correction.
    Pity me then, dear friend, and I assure ye,
    Even that your pity is enough to cure me.

112

Your love and pity doth th'impression[1] fill
Which vulgar scandal[2] stamped upon my brow;
For what care I who calls me well or ill
So you o'er-green[3] my bad, my good allow?
You are my all-the-world, and I must strive
To know my shames and praises from your tongue;
None else[4] to me, nor I to none alive,
That my steeled[5] sense o'er-changes right or wrong.
In so profound abysm I throw all care
Of others' voices, that my adder's sense[6]
To critic and to flatterer stoppèd are.
Mark how with my neglect I do dispense:
    You are so strongly in my purpose bred
    That all the world besides, methinks, are dead.

113

Since I left you, mine eye is in my mind,
And that which governs me to go about[1]
Doth part his function, and is partly blind;
Seems seeing, but effectually is out;[2]
For it no form delivers to the heart
Of bird, of flower, or shape which it doth latch;[3]
Of his quick objects[4] hath the mind no part,
Nor his own vision holds what it doth catch:
For if it[5] see the rud'st or gentlest sight,
The most sweet-favoured or deformed'st creature,
The mountain, or the sea, the day, or night,
The crow, or dove, it shapes them to your feature.
    Incapable of more, replete with you,
    My most true mind thus maketh mine untrue.[6]

114

Or whether[1] doth my mind, being crowned with you,
Drink up the monarch's plague, this flattery?
Or whether shall I say mine eye saith true,
And that your love taught it this alchemy,[2]
To make of monsters, and things indigest[3]
Such cherubins[4] as your sweet self resemble,
Creating every bad a perfect best
As fast as objects to his beams[5] assemble?
Oh, 'tis the first, 'tis flatt'ry in my seeing,
And my great mind most kingly drinks it up.
Mine eye well knows what with his gust[6] is 'greeing,
And to his palate doth prepare the cup.
    If it be poisoned, 'tis the lesser sin,
    That mine eye loves it and doth first begin.

115

Those lines that I before have writ do lie,
Even those that said I could not love you dearer;
Yet then my judgement knew no reason why
My most full flame should afterwards burn clearer.
But reckoning time, whose millioned accidents[1]
Creep in 'twixt vows, and change decrees of kings,
Tan[2] sacred beauty, blunt the sharp'st intents,
Divert strong minds to th'course of alt'ring things;[3]
Alas, why, fearing of time's tyranny,
Might I not then say, "Now I love you best",
When I was certain o'er incertainty,[4]
Crowning the present, doubting of the rest?
    Love is a babe;[5] then might I not say so,
      To give full growth to that which still doth grow?

116

Let me not to the marriage of true minds
Admit impediments;[1] love is not love
Which alters when it alteration finds,[2]
Or bends with the remover to remove.[3]
Oh no, it is an ever-fixèd mark,
That looks on tempests and is never shaken;
It is the star to every wand'ring bark,[4]
Whose worth's unknown, although his height be taken.[5]
Love's not Time's fool, though rosy lips and cheeks
Within his bending sickle's[6] compass come;
Love alters not with his brief hours and weeks,
But bears it out even to the edge of doom.
    If this be error and upon me proved,
      I never writ, nor no man ever loved.

117

Accuse me thus: that I have scanted[1] all
Wherein I should your great deserts[2] repay,
Forgot upon your dearest love to call,
Whereto all bonds do tie me day by day;
That I have frequent[3] been with unknown minds,
And given to time your own dear-purchased right;
That I have hoisted sail to all the winds
Which should transport me farthest from your sight.
Book[4] both my wilfulness and errors down,
And on just proof surmise accumulate;[5]
Bring me within the level[6] of your frown,
But shoot not at me in your wakened hate:
    Since my appeal[7] says I did strive to prove
    The constancy and virtue of your love.

118

Like as[1] to make our appetite more keen
With eager compounds[2] we our palate urge;
As, to prevent our maladies unseen,
We sicken to shun sickness when we purge;[3]
Even so, being full of your ne'er-cloying sweetness,
To bitter sauces did I frame my feeding,
And sick of welfare found a kind of meetness[4]
To be diseased ere that there was true needing.
Thus policy[5] in love, t'anticipate
The ills that were not, grew to faults assured,
And brought to medicine a healthful state
Which, rank of goodness,[6] would by ill be cured.
    But thence I learn, and find the lesson true,
    Drugs[7] poison him that so fell sick of you.

119

What potions have I drunk of siren[1] tears
Distilled from limbecks[2] foul as hell within,
Applying fears to hopes, and hopes to fears,
Still[3] losing when I saw myself to win!
What wretched errors hath my heart committed,
Whilst it hath thought itself so blessèd never!
How have mine eyes out of their spheres been fitted[4]
In the distraction of this madding fever!
O benefit of ill: now I find true
That better is by evil still made better,
And ruined love when it is built anew
Grows fairer than at first, more strong, far greater.
 So I return rebuked to my content,
 And gain by ills thrice more than I have spent.

120

That you were once unkind befriends[1] me now,
And for that sorrow, which I then did feel,
Needs must I under my transgression bow,[2]
Unless my nerves were brass or hammered steel.
For if you were by my unkindness shaken,
As I by yours, you've passed a hell of time,
And I, a tyrant, have no leisure taken[3]
To weigh[4] how once I suffered in your crime.
O that our night of woe might have remembered[5]
My deepest sense how hard true sorrow hits,
And soon to you, as you to me then, tendered[6]
The humble salve[7] which wounded bosoms fits!
 But that your trespass[8] now becomes a fee;
 Mine ransoms yours, and yours must ransom me.

121

'Tis better to be vile than vile esteemed,
When not to be, receives reproach of being,
And the just pleasure lost, which is so deemed
Not by our feeling, but by others' seeing.[1]
For why should others' false adulterate eyes[2]
Give salutation to my sportive blood?[3]
Or on my frailties why are frailer spies,
Which in their wills count bad what I think good?
No, I am that I am, and they that level[4]
At my abuses, reckon up their own;
I may be straight, though they themselves be bevel.[5]
By their rank[6] thoughts my deeds must not be shown,
 Unless this general evil they maintain:
 All men are bad, and in their badness reign.

122

Thy gift, thy tables,[1] are within my brain
Full charactered[2] with lasting memory,
Which shall above that idle rank[3] remain
Beyond all date, even to eternity—
Or at the least, so long as brain and heart
Have faculty by nature to subsist;
Till each[4] to razed oblivion yield his part
Of thee, thy record never can be missed.
That poor retention[5] could not so much hold,
Nor need I tallies thy dear love to score;[6]
Therefore to give them from me was I bold,
To trust those tables that receive thee more.
 To keep an adjunct to remember thee
 Were to import[7] forgetfulness in me.

123

No! Time, thou shalt not boast that I do change.
Thy pyramids, built up with newer might,[1]
To me are nothing novel, nothing strange;
They are but dressings of a former sight.
Our dates are brief,[2] and therefore we admire
What thou[3] dost foist upon us that is old,
And rather make them born to our desire
Than think that we before have heard them told.
Thy registers[4] and thee I both defy,
Not wond'ring at the present, nor the past,
For thy records, and what we see doth lie,
Made more or less by thy continual haste:
    This I do vow, and this shall ever be,
    I will be true despite thy scythe and thee.

124

If my dear love[1] were but the child of state[2]
It might for Fortune's bastard be unfathered,[3]
As subject to time's love or to time's hate,
Weeds among weeds, or flowers with flowers gathered.
No, it was builded far from accident;
It suffers not in smiling pomp,[4] nor falls
Under the blow of thrallèd discontent,[5]
Whereto th'inviting time our fashion calls:[6]
It fears not policy,[7] that heretic,
Which works on leases of short-numbered hours,
But all alone stands hugely politic,[8]
That it nor[9] grows with heat, nor drowns with showers.
    To this I witness call the fools of time,[10]
    Which die for goodness, who have lived for crime.

125

Were't aught[1] to me I bore the canopy,[2]
With my extern the outward honouring,[3]
Or laid great bases[4] for eternity,
Which proves more short than waste or ruining?
Have I not seen dwellers on form and favour[5]
Lose all, and more, by paying too much rent,[6]
For compound sweet forgoing simple savour,[7]
Pitiful thrivers, in their gazing spent?[8]
No, let me be obsequious[9] in thy heart,
And take thou my oblation,[10] poor but free,
Which is not mixed with seconds,[11] knows no art,
But mutual render,[12] only me for thee.
    Hence, thou suborned informer,[13] a true soul
      When most impeached, stands least in thy control.

126[1]

O thou my lovely boy who in thy power
Dost hold time's fickle glass,[2] his sickle hour,
Who hast by waning grown,[3] and therein show'st
Thy lovers withering, as thy sweet self grow'st.
If Nature, sovereign mistress over wrack,[4]
As thou goest onwards still[5] will pluck thee back,
She keeps thee to this purpose, that her skill
May time disgrace, and wretched minutes kill.
Yet fear her, O thou minion[6] of her pleasure:
She may detain, but not still[7] keep, her treasure!
    Her audit,[8] though delayed, answered must be,
      And her quietus[9] is to render thee.[10]

127[1]

In the old age[2] black was not counted fair,
Or if it were, it bore not beauty's name;
But now is black beauty's successive heir,[3]
And beauty[4] slandered with a bastard[5] shame.
For since each hand hath put on nature's power,
Fairing the foul with art's false borrowed face,[6]
Sweet beauty hath no name, no holy bower,[7]
But is profaned, if not lives in disgrace.
Therefore my mistress' eyes are raven black,
Her eyes so suited, and they mourners seem
At such who, not born fair, no beauty lack,
Sland'ring creation with a false esteem.[8]
 Yet so they[9] mourn, becoming of[10] their woe,
 That every tongue says beauty should look so.

128[1]

How oft when thou, my music,[2] music play'st
Upon that blessed wood[3] whose motion sounds
With thy sweet fingers, when thou gently sway'st
The wiry concord[4] that mine ear confounds,
Do I envy those jacks[5] that nimble leap,
To kiss the tender inward of thy hand,
Whilst my poor lips, which should that harvest reap,
At the wood's boldness by thee blushing stand!
To be so tickled they would change their state
And situation with those dancing chips,[6]
O'er whom thy fingers walk with gentle gait,
Making dead wood more blessed than living lips.
    Since saucy jacks[7] so happy are in this,
    Give them thy fingers, me thy lips to kiss.

129[1]

Th'expense of spirit[2] in a waste[3] of shame
Is lust in action; and till action, lust
Is perjured, murd'rous, bloody, full of blame,
Savage, extreme, rude, cruel, not to trust;
Enjoyed no sooner but despisèd straight;
Past reason hunted, and no sooner had,
Past reason hated as a swallowed bait
On purpose laid to make the taker mad;
Mad in pursuit, and in possession so;
Had, having, and in quest to have, extreme;
A bliss in proof, and proved, a very woe;
Before, a joy proposed; behind, a dream.
    All this the world well knows, yet none knows well
    To shun the heaven that leads men to this hell.

130[1]

My mistress' eyes are nothing like the sun;
Coral is far more red than her lips' red;
If snow be white, why then her breasts are dun;[2]
If hairs be wires,[3] black wires grow on her head;
I have seen roses damasked,[4] red and white,
But no such roses see I in her cheeks;
And in some perfumes is there more delight
Than in the breath that from my mistress reeks.
I love to hear her speak, yet well I know
That music hath a far more pleasing sound;
I grant I never saw a goddess go[5]—
My mistress when she walks treads on the ground.
    And yet, by heaven, I think my love as rare
    As any she belied with false compare.

131

Thou art as tyrannous, so as thou art,[1]
As those whose beauties proudly make them cruel;
For well thou know'st to my dear doting heart
Thou art the fairest and most precious jewel.
Yet in good faith some say, that thee behold,
Thy face hath not the power to make love groan;
To say they err, I dare not be so bold,
Although I swear it to myself alone.
And to be sure that is not false, I swear
A thousand groans but[2] thinking on thy face;
One on another's neck[3] do witness bear
Thy black is fairest in my judgement's place.
    In nothing art thou black save in thy deeds,
    And thence this slander, as I think, proceeds.

132

Thine eyes I love, and they, as pitying me,
Knowing thy heart torment[1] me with disdain,
Have put on black, and loving mourners be,
Looking with pretty ruth[2] upon my pain.
And truly, not the morning sun of heaven
Better becomes[3] the grey cheeks of the East,
Nor that full star that ushers in the even
Doth half that glory to the sober West
As those two mourning eyes become thy face:
Oh, let it then as well beseem[4] thy heart
To mourn for me, since mourning doth thee grace,
And suit[5] thy pity like in every part.
    Then will I swear beauty herself is black,
    And all they foul that thy complexion lack.

133[1]

Beshrew[2] that heart that makes my heart to groan
For that deep wound it gives my friend and me;
Is't not enough to torture me alone,
But slave to slavery[3] my sweet'st friend must be?
Me from myself thy cruel eye hath taken,
And my next self[4] thou harder hast engrossed.[5]
Of him, myself, and thee I am forsaken,
A torment thrice threefold thus to be crossed.[6]
Prison my heart in thy steel bosom's ward;[7]
But then my friend's heart let my poor heart bail.
Whoe'er keeps me, let my heart be his guard;
Thou canst not then use rigour in my jail.
    And yet thou wilt, for I being pent[8] in thee,
    Perforce am thine, and all that is in me.

134

So now I have confessed that he is thine,
And I myself am mortgaged to thy will,[1]
Myself I'll forfeit, so that other mine[2]
Thou wilt restore to be my comfort still;
But thou wilt not, nor he will not be free,
For thou art covetous, and he is kind;
He learned but surety-like to write[3] for me,
Under that bond that him as fast doth bind.
The statute of thy beauty thou wilt take,
Thou usurer, that put'st forth all to use,[4]
And sue a friend, came debtor for my sake;
So him I lose through my unkind abuse.
    Him have I lost; thou hast both him and me;
    He pays the whole, and yet am I not free.

135[1]

Whoever hath her wish, thou hast thy Will,
And Will to boot, and Will in overplus;
More than enough am I, that vex thee still,
To thy sweet will making addition thus.[2]
Wilt thou, whose will is large and spacious,
Not once vouchsafe to hide my will in thine?[3]
Shall will in others seem right gracious,
And in my will no fair acceptance shine?
The sea, all water, yet receives rain still,
And in abundance addeth to his store;
So thou, being rich in Will, add to thy Will
One will of mine, to make thy large Will more.
    Let no unkind no fair beseechers kill;[4]
    Think all but one, and me in that one Will.

136

If thy soul check[1] thee that I come so near,[2]
Swear to thy blind[3] soul that I was thy Will,
And will, thy soul knows, is admitted there;
Thus far for love my love-suit sweet fulfil.
Will will fulfil the treasure[4] of thy love,
Ay, fill it full with wills, and my will one;
In things of great receipt[5] with ease we prove
Among a number one is reckoned none.[6]
Then in the number let me pass untold,
Though in thy store's account I one must be.
For nothing hold me,[7] so it please thee hold
That nothing, me, a something sweet to thee.
    Make but my name thy love, and love that still,
    And then thou lov'st me, for my name is Will.

137

Thou blind fool, Love,[1] what dost thou to mine eyes,
That they behold, and see not what they see?
They know what beauty is, see where it lies,
Yet what the best is, take the worst to be.
If eyes, corrupt by over-partial[2] looks,
Be anchored in the bay where all men ride,[3]
Why of eyes' falsehood hast thou forgèd hooks,
Whereto the judgement of my heart is tied?
Why should my heart think that a several[4] plot
Which my heart knows the wide world's common place?
Or mine eyes, seeing this, say this is not,
To put fair truth upon so foul a face?
    In things right true my heart and eyes have erred,
    And to this false plague are they now transferred.

138[1]

When my love swears that she is made of truth,
I do believe her, though I know she lies,
That she might think me some untutored youth
Unlearnèd in the world's false subtleties.
Thus vainly thinking[2] that she thinks me young,
Although she knows my days are past the best,
Simply I credit[3] her false-speaking tongue;
On both sides thus is simple truth suppressed.
But wherefore[4] says she not she is unjust?
And wherefore say not I that I am old?
O love's best habit is in seeming trust,
And age in love loves not to have years told.[5]
 Therefore I lie[6] with her, and she with me,
 And in our faults by lies we flattered be.

139

O call not me to justify the wrong
That thy unkindness lays upon my heart;[1]
Wound me not with thine eye but with thy tongue;
Use power with power, and slay me not by art.[2]
Tell me thou lov'st elsewhere; but in my sight,
Dear heart, forbear to glance thine eye aside.
What need'st thou wound with cunning, when thy might
Is more than my o'erpressed defence can bide?
Let me excuse thee:[3] ah, my love well knows
Her pretty looks[4] have been mine enemies,
And therefore from my face she turns my foes
That they elsewhere might dart their injuries.
 Yet do not so, but since I am near slain,
 Kill me outright with looks, and rid my pain.

140

Be wise as thou art cruel, do not press
My tongue-tied patience with too much disdain,
Lest sorrow lend me words, and words express
The manner of my pity-wanting[1] pain.
If I might teach thee wit, better it were,
Though not to love, yet love to tell me so,[2]
As testy[3] sick men, when their deaths be near,
No news but health from their physicians know.
For if I should despair, I should grow mad,
And in my madness might speak ill of thee;
Now this ill-wresting[4] world is grown so bad,
Mad slanderers by mad ears believed be.
    That I may not be so, nor thou belied,
    Bear thine eyes straight,[5] though thy proud heart go wide.

141

In faith, I do not love thee with mine eyes,
For they in thee a thousand errors note;
But 'tis my heart that loves what they despise,
Who in despite of view is pleased to dote.[1]
Nor are mine ears with thy tongue's tune delighted,
Nor tender feeling to base touches prone,[2]
Nor taste, nor smell, desire to be invited
To any sensual feast with thee alone:
But my five wits,[3] nor my five senses, can
Dissuade one foolish heart from serving thee,
Who leaves unswayed the likeness of a man,[4]
Thy proud heart's slave and vassal wretch to be:
    Only my plague thus far I count my gain,
    That she that makes me sin, awards me pain.

142

Love is my sin, and thy dear virtue hate,[1]
Hate of my sin, grounded on sinful loving;
Oh, but with mine compare thou thine own state,
And thou shalt find it merits not reproving;
Or if it do, not from those lips of thine,
That have profaned their scarlet ornaments,[2]
And sealed false bonds of love as oft as mine,
Robbed others' beds' revenues of their rents.[3]
Be it lawful I love thee as thou lov'st those
Whom thine eyes woo, as mine importune[4] thee,
Root pity in thy heart, that when it grows,
Thy pity may deserve[5] to pitied be.
    If thou dost seek to have what thou dost hide,[6]
    By self-example mayst thou be denied.

143[1]

Lo, as a careful housewife runs to catch
One of her feathered creatures[2] broke away,
Sets down her babe, and makes all swift dispatch
In pursuit of the thing she would have stay;
Whilst her neglected child holds her in chase,
Cries to catch her whose busy care is bent
To follow that which flies before her face,
Not prizing her poor infant's discontent:
So run'st thou after that which flies from thee,
Whilst I, thy babe, chase thee afar behind.
But if thou catch thy hope, turn back to me,
And play the mother's part, kiss me, be kind.
    So will I pray that thou mayst have thy Will,
    If thou turn back and my loud crying still.[3]

144[1]

Two loves I have, of comfort and despair,[2]
Which, like two spirits, do suggest[3] me still:
The better angel is a man right fair,
The worser spirit a woman coloured ill.
To win me soon to hell my female evil
Tempteth my better angel from my side,
And would corrupt my saint to be a devil,
Wooing his purity with her foul pride.
And whether that my angel be turned fiend[4]
Suspect I may, yet not directly tell;
But being both from me,[5] both to each friend,
I guess one angel in another's hell.[6]
    Yet this shall I ne'er know, but live in doubt,
    Till my bad angel fire[7] my good one out.

145[1]

Those lips that Love's own hand did make
Breathed forth the sound that said "I hate",
To me, that languished for her sake;
But when she saw my woeful state,
Straight in her heart did mercy come,
Chiding that tongue that, ever sweet,
Was used in giving gentle doom,[2]
And taught it thus anew to greet:
"I hate" she altered with an end
That followed it as gentle day
Doth follow night who, like a fiend,
From heaven to hell is flown away.
    "I hate" from "hate" away she threw,
    And saved my life, saying "not you".

146[1]

Poor soul, the centre of my sinful earth,[2]
Thrall to[3] these rebel powers that thee array,[4]
Why dost thou pine within and suffer dearth,
Painting thy outward walls so costly gay?[5]
Why so large cost, having so short a lease,
Dost thou upon thy fading mansion[6] spend?
Shall worms, inheritors of this excess,
Eat up thy charge? Is this thy body's end?
Then soul, live thou upon thy servant's[7] loss,
And let that pine to aggravate thy store;
Buy terms divine in selling hours of dross,[8]
Within be fed, without be rich no more.
    So shalt thou feed on death, that feeds on men,
    And death once dead, there's no more dying then.

147

My love is as a fever, longing still
For that which longer nurseth the disease,
Feeding on that which doth preserve the ill,
Th'uncertain[1] sickly appetite to please:
My reason, the physician to my love,
Angry that his prescriptions are not kept,
Hath left me, and I desperate[2] now approve[3]
Desire is death, which physic did except.[4]
Past cure I am, now reason is past care,
And frantic-mad with evermore unrest,
My thoughts and my discourse as madmen's are,
At random from the truth vainly expressed.
    For I have sworn thee fair, and thought thee bright,
    Who art as black as hell, as dark as night.

148

O me! What eyes hath love put in my head,
Which have no correspondence[1] with true sight?
Or if they have, where is my judgement fled,
That censures[2] falsely what they see aright?
If that be fair whereon my false eyes dote,
What means the world to say it is not so?
If it be not, then love doth well denote,
Love's eye is not so true as all men's no,
How can it? O how can love's eye be true,
That is so vexed with watching[3] and with tears?
No marvel then though I mistake my view:
The sun itself sees not, till heaven clears.
    O cunning love, with tears thou keep'st me blind,
    Lest eyes well-seeing thy foul faults should find.

149

Canst thou, O cruel, say I love thee not,
When I against myself with thee partake?[1]
Do I not think on thee, when I forgot
Am of myself—all, tyrant, for thy sake?
Who hateth thee, that I do call my friend?
On whom frown'st thou, that I do fawn upon?
Nay, if thou lour'st[2] on me, do I not spend
Revenge upon myself with present moan?[3]
What merit do I in myself respect[4]
That is so proud thy service to despise,
When all my best doth worship thy defect,
Commanded by the motion of thine eyes?
    But, love, hate on, for now I know thy mind:
    Those that can see thou lov'st, and I am blind.

150

O from what power hast thou this powerful might,
With insufficiency[1] my heart to sway,
To make me give the lie to my true sight,
And swear that brightness[2] doth not grace the day?
Whence hast thou this becoming[3] of things ill,
That in the very refuse of thy deeds
There is such strength and warrantise[4] of skill
That in my mind thy worst all best exceeds?[5]
Who taught thee how to make me love thee more,
The more I hear and see just cause of hate?
Oh, though I love what others do abhor,
With others thou shouldst not abhor my state.
    If thy unworthiness raised love in me,
    More worthy I to be beloved of thee.

151

Love is too young[1] to know what conscience is;
Yet who knows not conscience[2] is born of love?
Then, gentle cheater, urge not my amiss,
Lest guilty of my faults thy sweet self prove.
For, thou betraying me, I do betray
My nobler part[3] to my gross body's treason;
My soul doth tell my body that he may
Triumph in love; flesh stays no farther reason,
But rising[4] at thy name doth point out thee
As his triumphant prize. Proud of[5] this pride,
He is contented thy poor drudge to be,
To stand in thy affairs, fall by thy side.
 No want of conscience hold it that I call
 Her "love", for whose dear love I rise and fall.

152

In loving thee thou know'st I am forsworn,[1]
But thou art twice forsworn to me love swearing,
In act thy bed-vow broke and new faith torn,
In vowing new hate after new love bearing.
But why of two oaths' breach do I accuse thee,
When I break twenty? I am perjured most,
For all my vows are oaths but to misuse thee,
And all my honest faith in thee is lost.
For I have sworn deep oaths of thy deep kindness,
Oaths of thy love, thy truth, thy constancy,
And to enlighten thee gave eyes to blindness,
Or made them swear against the thing they see.
 For I have sworn thee fair: more perjured eye,
 To swear against the truth so foul a lie.

153[1]

Cupid laid by his brand,[2] and fell asleep;
A maid of Dian's[3] this advantage found,
And his love-kindling fire did quickly steep
In a cold valley-fountain of that ground,[4]
Which borrowed from this holy fire of Love
A dateless lively heat still to endure,
And grew a seething[5] bath, which yet men prove
Against strange maladies a sovereign[6] cure:
But at my mistress' eye Love's brand new-fired,
The boy for trial[7] needs would touch my breast;
I, sick withal, the help of bath desired,
And thither hied,[8] a sad distempered[9] guest,
    But found no cure; the bath for my help lies
    Where Cupid got new fire—my mistress' eyes.

154

The little love-god lying once asleep,
Laid by his side his heart-inflaming brand,
Whilst many nymphs that vowed chaste life to keep
Came tripping by, but in her maiden hand
The fairest votary[1] took up that fire
Which many legions of true hearts had warmed;
And so the general[2] of hot desire
Was, sleeping, by a virgin hand disarmed.
This brand she quenched in a cool well by,
Which from Love's fire took heat perpetual,
Growing a bath and healthful remedy
For men diseased, but I, my mistress' thrall,
    Came there for cure, and this by that I prove:
    Love's fire heats water, water cools not love.

2

Venus and Adonis

If any being, mortal or immortal, could find her way along the course of true love, surely it would be Venus, goddess of love. Yet *Venus and Adonis*, Shakespeare's first publication, celebrates a mythical event in which even she is defeated. Adonis is a beautiful and adventurous young man, setting out to hunt the dangerous boar. Despite Venus's evident attractions, Adonis, like a modern teenager perhaps, is more interested in his peer group and the thrill of danger than in love; he refuses her advances, goes hunting instead, and is fatally gored.

Venus and Adonis was carefully prepared for the press, and was dedicated to the Earl of Southampton. The poem was immensely popular with its readers: there were many early editions; and a play of the period has a character, an undergraduate at Cambridge, worshipping, "sweet Mr Shakespeare" and laying "his *Venus and Adonis* under [his] pillow".[1]

The poem explores both the excitement and the comedy of sexuality. The situation is, perhaps, something of a young man's fantasy, as a beautiful boy is wooed by a goddess, and has the power to refuse her advances. It is true, however, that while Venus is comical (she sweats in the heat of the day), she is also portrayed with sympathy, especially when, at the climax of the poem, she sees the slain Adonis. At this point the poem becomes something of a creation myth (see Introduction, pp.6–7), as Venus prophesies that the nature of love will from henceforth be troubled, and that "Sorrow on love hereafter shall attend".

[**Note:** Not all of the original poem is reproduced here and the removal of verses is marked as a break by the insertion of . . . .]

Even as the sun with purple-coloured face
Had ta'en his last leave of the weeping morn,
Rose-cheeked Adonis hied him to the chase;
Hunting he loved, but love he laughed to scorn.
    Sick-thoughted Venus makes amain[2] unto him,
    And like a bold-faced suitor 'gins[3] to woo him.

"Thrice fairer than myself," thus she began,
"The field's chief flower, sweet above compare,
Stain to all nymphs,[4] more lovely than a man,
More white and red than doves or roses are;
    Nature that made thee with herself at strife
    Saith[5] that the world hath ending with thy life.

"Vouchsafe, thou wonder, to alight thy steed,
And rein his proud head to the saddle-bow;
If thou wilt deign this favour, for thy meed[6]
A thousand honey secrets shalt thou know.
    Here come and sit, where never serpent hisses,
    And being set, I'll smother thee with kisses;

"And yet not cloy thy lips with loathed saiety,
But rather famish them amid their plenty,
Making them red and pale with fresh variety;
Ten kisses short as one, one long as twenty.
    A summer's day will seem an hour but short,
    Being wasted in such time-beguiling sport."

With this she seizeth on his sweating palm,
The precedent of pith and livelihood,
And, trembling in her passion, calls it balm,
Earth's sovereign salve to do a goddess good.

Being so enraged, desire doth lend her force
Courageously to pluck him from his horse.

Over one arm the lusty courser's rein,
Under her other was the tender boy,
Who blushed and pouted in a dull disdain,
With leaden appetite, unapt to toy;
    She red and hot as coals of glowing fire,
    He red for shame, but frosty in desire.

The studded bridle on a ragged bough
Nimbly she fastens—O, how quick is love!
The steed is stalled up, and even now
To tie the rider she begins to prove.
    Backward she pushed him, as she would be thrust,
    And governed him in strength, though not in lust.

. . . .

"Fondling", she saith, "since I have hemmed thee here
Within the circuit of this ivory pale,[7]
I'll be a park, and thou shalt be my deer;
Feed where thou wilt, on mountain or in dale;
    Graze on my lips, and if those hills be dry,
    Stray lower, where the pleasant fountains lie.

"Within this limit is relief enough,
Sweet bottom-grass[8] and high delightful plain,
Round rising hillocks, brakes obscure and rough,
To shelter thee from tempest and from rain:
    Then be my deer, since I am such a park;
    No dog shall rouse thee, though a thousand bark."

At this Adonis smiles as in disdain,

That in each cheek appears a pretty dimple.
Love made those hollows, if himself were slain,
He might be buried in a tomb so simple;
    Foreknowing well, if there he came to lie,
      Why, there Love lived, and there he could not die.

These lovely caves, these round enchanting pits,
Opened their mouths to swallow Venus' liking.
Being mad before, how doth she now for wits?
Struck dead at first, what needs a second striking?
    Poor queen of love, in thine own law forlorn,
      To love a cheek that smiles at thee in scorn!

        . . . .

Now was she just before him as he sat,
And like a lowly lover down she kneels;
With one fair hand she heaveth up his hat,
Her other tender hand his fair cheek feels;
    His tenderer cheek receives her soft hand's print
      As apt as new-fallen snow takes any dint.

O, what a war of looks was then between them,
Her eyes petitioners to his eyes suing!
His eyes saw her eyes as they had not seen them;
Her eyes wooed still, his eyes disdained the wooing;
    And all this dumb play had his acts made plain[9]
      With tears which chorus-like her eyes did rain.

Full gently now she takes him by the hand,
A lily prisoned in a jail of snow,
Or ivory in an alabaster band;
So white a friend engirts[10] so white a foe:
    This beauteous combat, wilful and unwilling,

Showed like two silver doves that sit a-billing.

. . . .

"Sweet boy", she says, "this night I'll waste in sorrow,
For my sick heart commands mine eyes to watch.[11]
Tell me, love's master, shall we meet to-morrow?
Say, shall we? Shall we? Wilt thou make the match?"
    He tells her no: to-morrow he intends
    To hunt the boar with certain of his friends.

"The boar!" quoth she: whereat a sudden pale,
Like lawn being spread upon the blushing rose,
Usurps her cheek; she trembles at his tale,
And on his neck her yoking arms she throws.
    She sinketh down, still hanging by his neck,
    He on her belly falls, she on her back.

Now is she in the very lists of love,
Her champion mounted for the hot encounter.
All is imaginary she doth prove;[12]
He will not manage her, although he mount her;
    That worse than Tantalus' is her annoy,[13]
    To clip Elysium[14] and to lack her joy.

Even so poor birds, deceived with painted grapes,
Do surfeit by the eye and pine the maw;[15]
Even so she languisheth in her mishaps
As those poor birds that helpless berries saw.
    The warm effects which she in him finds missing
    She seeks to kindle with continual kissing.

But all in vain, good queen, it will not be.
She hath assayed as much as may be proved;

Her pleading hath deserved a greater fee;
She's Love, she loves, and yet she is not loved.
  "Fie, fie," he says, "you crush me; let me go;
  You have no reason to withhold me so."

"Thou hadst been gone," quoth she, "sweet boy, ere this,
But that thou told'st me thou wouldst hunt the boar.
O, be advised: thou know'st not what it is
With javelin's point a churlish swine to gore,
  Whose tushes[16] never sheathed he whetteth still,
  Like to a mortal butcher bent to kill."
                        . . . .
"Nay, then," quoth Adon, "you will fall again
Into your idle over-handled[17] theme.
The kiss I gave you is bestowed in vain,
And all in vain you strive against the stream;
  For by this black-faced night, desire's foul nurse,
  Your treatise makes me like you worse and worse.
                        . . . .
"What have you urged that I cannot reprove?
The path is smooth that leadeth on to danger;
I hate not love, but your device in love
That lends embracements unto every stranger.
  You do it for increase: O strange excuse,
  When reason is the bawd to lust's abuse!

"Call it not love, for Love to heaven is fled
Since sweating Lust on earth usurped his name;
Under whose simple semblance he hath fed
Upon fresh beauty, blotting it with blame;
  Which the hot tyrant stains and soon bereaves,
  As caterpillars do the tender leaves.

"Love comforteth like sunshine after rain,
But Lust's effect is tempest after sun;
Love's gentle spring doth always fresh remain,
Lust's winter comes ere summer half be done;
    Love surfeits not, Lust like a glutton dies;
    Love is all truth, Lust full of forged lies.

"More I could tell, but more I dare not say;
The text is old, the orator too green.[18]
Therefore, in sadness,[19] now I will away;
My face is full of shame, my heart of teen:[20]
    Mine ears that to your wanton talk attended
    Do burn themselves for having so offended."

With this, he breaketh from the sweet embrace
Of those fair arms which bound him to her breast,
And homeward through the dark laund[21] runs apace;
Leaves Love upon her back deeply distressed.
    Look how a bright star shooteth from the sky,
    So glides he in the night from Venus' eye;

Which after him she darts, as one on shore
Gazing upon a late-embarkèd friend,
Till the wild waves will have him seen no more,
Whose ridges with the meeting clouds contend;
    So did the merciless and pitchy night
    Fold in the object that did feed her sight.

Thus Adonis breaks away from Venus and heads for the hunt.
Venus, pursuing him, hears the baying of the hounds and follows
the sound in the hope of seeing Adonis once more.

As falcons to the lure, away she flies;
The grass stoops not, she treads on it so light;
And in her haste unfortunately spies
The foul boar's conquest on her fair delight;
    Which seen, her eyes, as murdered with the view,
    Like stars ashamed of day, themselves withdrew;

Or as the snail, whose tender horns being hit,
Shrinks backward in his shelly cave with pain,
And there all smothered up in shade doth sit,
Long after fearing to creep forth again;
    So at his bloody view her eyes are fled
    Into the deep-dark cabins of her head.

. . . .

Upon his hurt she looks so steadfastly
That her sight, dazzling, makes the wound seem three;
And then she reprehends her mangling eye
That makes more gashes where no breach should be:
    His face seems twain, each several[22] limb is doubled;
    For oft the eye mistakes, the brain being troubled.

"My tongue cannot express my grief for one,
And yet," quoth she, "behold two Adons dead!
My sighs are blown away, my salt tears gone,
Mine eyes are turned to fire, my heart to lead;
    Heavy heart's lead, melt at mine eyes' red fire!
    So shall I die by drops of hot desire.

. . . .

"'Tis true, 'tis true; thus was Adonis slain:
He ran upon the boar with his sharp spear,
Who did not whet his teeth at him again,
But by a kiss thought to persuade him there;

And nuzzling in his flank, the loving swine
Sheathed unaware the tusk in his soft groin.

"Had I been toothed like him, I must confess,
With kissing him I should have killed him first;
But he is dead, and never did he bless
My youth with his; the more am I accurst."
    With this, she falleth in the place she stood,
    And stains her face with his congealed blood.

She looks upon his lips, and they are pale;
She takes him by the hand, and that is cold;
She whispers in his ears a heavy tale,
As if they heard the woeful words she told;
    She lifts the coffer-lids[23] that close his eyes,
    Where, lo, two lamps, burnt out, in darkness lies;

Two glasses, where herself herself beheld
A thousand times, and now no more, reflect;
Their virtue lost wherein they late excelled,
And every beauty robbed of his effect.
    "Wonder of time," quoth she, "this is my spite,
    That, thou being dead, the day should yet be light.

"Since thou art dead, lo, here I prophesy
Sorrow on love hereafter shall attend;
It shall be waited on with jealousy,
Find sweet beginning but unsavoury end;
    Ne'er settled equally, but high or low,
    That all love's pleasure shall not match his woe.

"It shall be fickle, false and full of fraud;

Bud, and be blasted,[24] in a breathing while;
The bottom poison, and the top o'erstrawed[25]
With sweets that shall the truest sight beguile;
    The strongest body shall it make most weak,
    Strike the wise dumb, and teach the fool to speak.

"It shall be sparing, and too full of riot,
Teaching decrepit age to tread the measures;
The staring ruffian shall it keep in quiet,
Pluck down the rich, enrich the poor with treasures;
    It shall be raging-mad, and silly-mild,
    Make the young old, the old become a child.

"It shall suspect where is no cause of fear;
It shall not fear where it should most mistrust;
It shall be merciful and too severe,
And most deceiving when it seems most just;
    Perverse it shall be where it shows most toward,
    Put fear to valour, courage to the coward.

"It shall be cause of war and dire events,
And set dissension 'twixt the son and sire;
Subject and servile to all discontents,
As dry combustious matter is to fire.
    Sith in his prime death doth my love destroy,
    They that love best their loves shall not enjoy."

By this the boy that by her side lay killed
Was melted like a vapour from her sight,
And in his blood that on the ground lay spilled
A purple flower sprung up, chequered with white,
    Resembling well his pale cheeks, and the blood

Which in round drops upon their whiteness stood.

She bows her head the new-sprung flower to smell,
Comparing it to her Adonis' breath;
And says within her bosom it shall dwell,
Since he himself is reft from her by death;
    She crops the stalk, and in the breach appears
    Green-dropping sap, which she compares to tears.

"Poor flower," quoth she, "this was thy father's guise
Sweet issue of a more sweet-smelling sire
For every little grief to wet his eyes.
To grow unto himself was his desire,
    And so 'tis thine; but know, it is as good
    To wither in my breast as in his blood.

"Here was thy father's bed, here in my breast;
Thou art the next of blood, and 'tis thy right.
Lo, in this hollow cradle take thy rest;
My throbbing heart shall rock thee day and night;
    There shall not be one minute in an hour
    Wherein I will not kiss my sweet love's flower."

Thus weary of the world, away she hies,
And yokes her silver doves, by whose swift aid
Their mistress, mounted, through the empty skies
In her light chariot quickly is conveyed,
    Holding their course to Paphos,[26] where their queen
    Means to immure[27] herself and not be seen.

WILLIAM SHAKESPEARE

PART TWO
Plays

GLOBE . SOUTHWARKE .

" our theators are rased downe
and where they

A Midsummer Night's Dream

As Shakespeare's plays and poems explore the art of love, they return insistently to the challenges that face lovers of all ages and persuasions. Love, especially young love, is ecstatic, but at the same time tenuous, brief, unrequited or resisted. In his comedies, tragedies and narrative poems, Shakespeare dramatizes the course of love in a variety of situations, from domestic to mythical; all his lovers face challenges, and none achieves unalloyed happiness.

In the comedy *A Midsummer Night's Dream*, only the intervention of Oberon, king of the fairies, can ensure a happy ending; he arranges through Puck that one of the lovers remains under the spell of a love-potion. The course of true love never did run smooth.

ACT 1, SCENE 1

LYSANDER	How now, my love! Why is your cheek so pale?
	How chance the roses there do fade so fast?
HERMIA	Belike[1] for want of rain, which I could well
	Beteem[2] them from the tempest of my eyes.
LYSANDER	Ay me, for aught that I could ever read,
	Could ever hear by tale or history,
	The course of true love never did run smooth;
	But either it was different in blood[3]—
HERMIA	O cross! too high to be enthralled to low.
LYSANDER	Or else misgrafted[4] in respect of years—
HERMIA	O spite! too old to be engaged to young.
LYSANDER	Or else it stood upon the choice of friends—
HERMIA	O hell! to choose love by another's eyes.
LYSANDER	Or, if there were a sympathy in choice,
	War, death, or sickness, did lay siege to it,

Making it momentary as a sound,
Swift as a shadow, short as any dream;
Brief as the lightning in the collied[5] night
That, in a spleen,[6] unfolds both heaven and earth,
And ere a man hath power to say "Behold!"
The jaws of darkness do devour it up:
So quick bright things come to confusion.

Love's Labour's Lost

Like *A Midsummer Night's Dream*, *Love's Labour's Lost* is an exuberant exploration of the excesses of young love. Shakespeare revels in the richness of language that he has been exploiting in the sonnets – the play actually includes several love sonnets in its dialogue. One of the minor characters of the play comments on the heightened rhetoric the others employ: "They have been at a great feast of languages and stolen the scraps." The play is full of rhyming passages, elaborate puns and inventive imagery.

The young King Ferdinand of Navarre and three of his friends have taken a vow to commit themselves to a celibate and ascetic life of study. Of course, just as the vow is complete, the princess of France and three ladies in waiting arrive to negotiate a pact with the king. Like a formal dance, the four young men fall in love with their respective ladies, while the women treat their attentions as a courtly joke.

Berowne is the most outspoken, sceptical and satirical of the four lords. Despite himself, he falls in love with Rosaline, a dark beauty. In this soliloquy, he castigates himself for being in love, and, in language reminiscent of the sonnets to the dark woman, he berates himself – and women in general. He is particularly bitter about the qualities of love figured in the image of Cupid: small, naked and blind, but immensely powerful over the human heart.

ACT 3, SCENE 1

BEROWNE   And I, forsooth, in love. I, that have been love's whip,

                A very beadle[1] to a humorous sigh,

                A critic, nay, a night-watch constable,

                A domineering pedant[2] o'er the boy,

                Than whom no mortal so magnificent!

This wimpled,[3] whining, purblind,[4] wayward boy,
This senior-junior, giant-dwarf, Dan[5] Cupid;
Regent of love-rhymes, lord of folded arms,[6]
Th' anointed sovereign of sighs and groans,
Liege of all loiterers and malcontents,
Dread prince of plackets, king of codpieces,[7]
Sole imperator and great general
Of trotting paritors[8]—O my little heart!
And I to be a corporal of his field,[9]
And wear his colours like a tumbler's hoop!
What? I love, I sue, I seek a wife—
A woman that is like a German clock,
Still a-repairing, ever out of frame
And never going aright; being a watch,
But being watched that it may still go right!
Nay, to be perjured, which is worst of all;
And, among three, to love the worst of all,
A whitely wanton with a velvet brow,
With two pitch-balls stuck in her face for eyes;
Ay, and by heaven, one that will do the deed,
Though Argus[10] were her eunuch and her guard.
And I to sigh for her, to watch for her,
To pray for her! Go to; it is a plague
That Cupid will impose for my neglect
Of his almighty dreadful little might.
    Well, I will love, write, sigh, pray, sue, and groan.
    Some men must love my lady, and some Joan.

Exit

Later, in a scene of high comedy, the four lovers each enter to read a sonnet they have written. As they do so, in turn they hide and spy on each other. Eventually they realize that they are all in love.

Berowne is the last to be discovered, whereupon he praises Rosaline extravagantly, and some competition ensues as the men each claim that their love is fairest. The king asks Berowne to rationalize their love: to prove their loving lawful and their faith not "torn", despite the fact that they have broken their vow. Berowne does so, reaching a climax in a glowingly rhetorical passage that proclaims the superior value of poetry – and love – over all other "arts".

ACT 4, SCENE 3

BEROWNE   Who sees the heavenly Rosaline
        That, like a rude and savage man of Ind[11]
           At the first opening of the gorgeous east,
        Bows not his vassal head and, strucken blind,
           Kisses the base ground with obedient breast?
        What peremptory eagle-sighted[12] eye
           Dares look upon the heaven of her brow
        That is not blinded by her majesty?

KING   What zeal, what fury hath inspired thee now?
        My love, her mistress, is a gracious moon;
           She, an attending star, scarce seen a light.

BEROWNE   My eyes are then no eyes, nor I Berowne.
           O, but for my love, day would turn to night!
        Of all complexions the culled sovereignty[13]
           Do meet, as at a fair, in her fair cheek,
        Where several worthies make one dignity,
           Where nothing wants[14] that want itself doth seek.
        Lend me the flourish of all gentle tongues—
           Fie, painted rhetoric![15] O, she needs it not.
        To things of sale a seller's praise belongs:
           She passes praise; then praise too short doth blot.
        A withered hermit, five-score[16] winters worn,
           Might shake off fifty, looking in her eye.

	Beauty doth varnish age, as if new born,
	And gives the crutch the cradle's infancy.
	O, 'tis the sun that maketh all things shine.
KING	By heaven, thy love is black as ebony.
BEROWNE	Is ebony like her? O word divine!
	A wife of such wood were felicity.
	O, who can give an oath? Where is a book?[17]
	That I may swear beauty doth beauty lack,
	If that she learn not of her eye to look.
	No face is fair that is not full so black.
KING	O paradox! Black is the badge of hell,
	The hue of dungeons and the school of night;
	And beauty's crest becomes the heavens well.[18]
BEROWNE	Devils soonest tempt, resembling spirits of light.
	O, if in black my lady's brows be decked,
	It mourns that painting and usurping hair[19]
	Should ravish doters with a false aspect;
	And therefore is she born to make black fair.
	Her favour turns the fashion of the days,
	For native blood is counted painting now;
	And therefore red, that would avoid dispraise,
	Paints itself black, to imitate her brow.
DUMAINE	To look like her are chimney-sweepers black.
LONGAVILLE	And since her time are colliers[20] counted bright.
KING	And Ethiopes of their sweet complexion crack.
DUMAINE	Dark needs no candles now, for dark is light.
BEROWNE	Your mistresses dare never come in rain,
	For fear their colours should be washed away.
KING	'Twere good yours did; for, sir, to tell you plain,
	I'll find a fairer face not washed today.
BEROWNE	I'll prove her fair, or talk till doomsday here.

· · · · · · · ·

KING	Then leave this chat; and, good Berowne, now prove
	Our loving lawful and our faith not torn.
DUMAINE	Ay, marry, there; some flattery for this evil.
LONGAVILLE	O, some authority how to proceed;
	Some tricks, some quillets,[21] how to cheat the devil!
DUMAINE	Some salve[22] for perjury.
BEROWNE	O, 'tis more than need.

Have at you then, affection's men-at-arms.

Consider what you first did swear unto:

To fast, to study, and to see no woman—

Flat treason 'gainst the kingly state of youth.

Say, can you fast? Your stomachs are too young,

And abstinence engenders maladies.

. . . .

O, we have made a vow to study, lords,

And in that vow we have forsworn our books.

For when would you, my liege, or you, or you,

In leaden contemplation have found out

Such fiery numbers[23] as the prompting eyes

Of beauty's tutors have enriched you with?

Other slow arts entirely keep the brain,

And therefore, finding barren practisers,

Scarce show a harvest of their heavy toil;

But love, first learned in a lady's eyes,

Lives not alone immured[24] in the brain,

But with the motion of all elements

Courses as swift as thought in every power,

And gives to every power a double power,

Above their functions and their offices.

It adds a precious seeing to the eye:

A lover's eyes will gaze an eagle blind.

A lover's ear will hear the lowest sound,
When the suspicious head of theft is stopped.[25]
Love's feeling is more soft and sensible
Than are the tender horns of cockled snails.[26]
Love's tongue proves dainty Bacchus[27] gross in taste;
For valour, is not Love a Hercules,
Still climbing trees in the Hesperides?[28]
Subtle as Sphinx,[29] as sweet and musical
As bright Apollo's lute,[30] strung with his hair.
And when Love speaks, the voice of all the gods
Make heaven drowsy with the harmony.
Never durst poet touch a pen to write
Until his ink were tempered with Love's sighs.
O, then his lines would ravish savage ears,
And plant in tyrants mild humility.
From women's eyes this doctrine I derive:
They sparkle still the right Promethean fire;[31]
They are the books, the arts, the academies,
That show, contain, and nourish all the world;
Else none at all in aught proves excellent.
Then fools you were these women to forswear;
Or, keeping what is sworn, you will prove fools.
For wisdom's sake, a word that all men love;
Or for Love's sake, a word that loves all men;
Or for men's sake, the authors of these women;
Or women's sake, by whom we men are men—
Let us once lose our oaths to find ourselves,
Or else we lose ourselves to keep our oaths.
It is religion to be thus forsworn,
For charity itself fulfils the law,
And who can sever love from charity?

KING   Saint Cupid, then! And, soldiers, to the field!

In the last act, the four men claim passionately that their love is genuine, but their protestations are cut short by one of Shakespeare's very few surprise endings: a messenger arrives out of the blue, announcing that the princess's father has died. The four men continue to plead their case, despite the distress of the princess. Berowne finally realizes the need for simplicity in language – though his facility in rationalization remains intact. The ladies partially relent, postponing the possible happy ending by a year to allow for mourning, and each setting their lover a task to be completed in that time.

ACT 5, SCENE 2

BEROWNE   Honest plain words best pierce the ear of grief;
And by these badges understand the King.
For your fair sakes have we neglected time,
Played foul play with our oaths. Your beauty, ladies,
Hath much deformed us, fashioning our humours
Even to the opposed end of our intents;
And what in us hath seemed ridiculous—
As love is full of unbefitting strains,
All wanton as a child, skipping and vain;
Formed by the eye and therefore, like the eye,
Full of strange shapes, of habits, and of forms,
Varying in subjects as the eye doth roll
To every varied object in his glance;
Which parti-coated presence of loose love
Put on by us, if, in your heavenly eyes
Have misbecomed our oaths and gravities,
Those heavenly eyes that look into these faults
Suggested us to make. Therefore, ladies,
Our love being yours, the error that love makes
Is likewise yours. We to ourselves prove false,

	By being once false for ever to be true
	To those that make us both—fair ladies, you;
	And even that falsehood, in itself a sin,
	Thus purifies itself and turns to grace.
PRINCESS	We have received your letters full of love,
	Your favours, the ambassadors of love,
	And in our maiden counsel rated them[32]
	At courtship, pleasant jest, and courtesy,
	As bombast and as lining[33] to the time.
	But more devout than this in our respects
	Have we not been; and therefore met your loves
	In their own fashion, like a merriment.
DUMAINE	Our letters, madam, showed much more than jest.
LONGAVILLE	So did our looks.
ROSALINE	We did not quote them so.
KING	Now, at the latest minute of the hour,
	Grant us your loves.
PRINCESS	A time, methinks, too short
	To make a world-without-end bargain in.

. . . .

BEROWNE	Studies my lady? Mistress, look on me.
	Behold the window of my heart, mine eye,
	What humble suit attends thy answer there.
	Impose some service on me for thy love.
ROSALINE	Oft have I heard of you, my Lord Berowne,
	Before I saw you; and the world's large tongue
	Proclaims you for a man replete with mocks,
	Full of comparisons and wounding flouts,[34]
	Which you on all estates[35] will execute
	That lie within the mercy of your wit.
	To weed this wormwood[36] from your fruitful brain
	And therewithal to win me, if you please—

Without the which I am not to be won—
You shall this twelvemonth term from day to day
Visit the speechless sick, and still converse
With groaning wretches; and your task shall be,
With all the fierce endeavour of your wit,
To enforce the pained impotent to smile.

BEROWNE   To move wild laughter in the throat of death?
It cannot be; it is impossible.
Mirth cannot move a soul in agony.

ROSALINE   Why, that's the way to choke a gibing spirit,
Whose influence is begot of that loose grace
Which shallow laughing hearers give to fools.
A jest's prosperity lies in the ear
Of him that hears it, never in the tongue
Of him that makes it. Then, if sickly ears,
Deafed with the clamours of their own dear groans,
Will hear your idle scorns, continue then,
And I will have you and that fault withal.
But, if they will not, throw away that spirit,
And I shall find you empty of that fault,
Right joyful of your reformation.

BEROWNE   A twelvemonth? Well, befall what will befall,
I'll jest a twelvemonth in an hospital.

PRINCESS   [To the King] Ay, sweet my lord, and so I take my
                       leave.

KING   No, madam, we will bring you on your way.

BEROWNE   Our wooing doth not end like an old play:
Jack hath not Jill. These ladies' courtesy
Might well have made our sport a comedy.

KING   Come, sir, it wants a twelvemonth and a day,
And then 'twill end.

BEROWNE   That's too long for a play.

AN
EXCELLENT
conceited Tragedie
OF
Romeo and Iuliet.

As it hath been often (with great applause)
plaid publiquely, by the right Honourable the L. of *Hunsdon*
his Seruants.

LONDON,
Printed by Iohn Danter.
1597

1

Romeo and Juliet

The story of Romeo and Juliet has become synonymous with passionate, tragic young love. It has been celebrated recently in movies from the ultra-modern *Romeo + Juliet* of Baz Luhrmann to the witty and inventive *Shakespeare in Love*.

Shakespeare creates lovers who are partly responsible for their own tragedies, but who are also dogged by sheer bad luck – the friar who was supposed to bring Romeo the news that Juliet had only faked her death is delayed by an outbreak of the plague – and they are surrounded by a society that is narcissistic and every bit as hasty in making decisions as the lovers. Although the play begins more like a comedy than a tragedy, at the end the friar's magic potion, inducing Juliet's seeming death, fails to make the course of true love run smooth.

Romeo begins by being in love with the wrong person, the unattainable Rosalind. His language is artificial, and full of traditional paradoxes.

ACT 1, SCENE 1

BENVOLIO	What sadness lengthens Romeo's hours?
ROMEO	Not having that which, having, makes them short.
BENVOLIO	In love?
ROMEO	Out.
BENVOLIO	Of love?
ROMEO	Out of her favour where I am in love.
BENVOLIO	Alas that love, so gentle in his view,
	Should be so tyrannous and rough in proof.
ROMEO	Alas that love, whose view is muffled[1] still,
	Should without eyes see pathways to his will.

Where shall we dine?² O me! What fray was here?
Yet tell me not, for I have heard it all.
Here's much to do with hate, but more with love.
Why then, O brawling love, O loving hate,
O anything, of nothing first create!
O heavy lightness, serious vanity,
Misshapen chaos of well-seeming forms!
Feather of lead, bright smoke, cold fire, sick health,
Still-waking sleep that is not what it is!
This love feel I, that feel no love in this. . . .
Love is a smoke made with the fume of sighs;
Being purged, a fire sparkling in lovers' eyes;
Being vexed, a sea nourished with lovers' tears.
What is it else? A madness most discreet,
A choking gall,³ and a preserving sweet.

Invited to a ball at the rival Capulet mansion, Romeo and his friends arrive in disguise. The first meeting between Romeo and Juliet is a dance of language, as they jointly compose a perfect sonnet. The pair are perfectly matched, as the younger Juliet is as adept at teasing as Romeo is at wooing.

ACT 1, SCENE 5

ROMEO   [*to a servingman*] What lady's that which doth enrich the hand
                Of yonder knight?

SERVANT   I know not, sir.

ROMEO   O, she doth teach the torches to burn bright.
                It seems she hangs upon the cheek of night
                As a rich jewel in an Ethiop's ear—
                Beauty too rich for use, for earth too dear.
                So shows a snowy dove trooping with crows

As yonder lady o'er her fellows shows.
The measure[4] done, I'll watch her place of stand,
And, touching hers, make blessèd my rude hand.
Did my heart love till now? Forswear[5] it, sight:
For I ne'er saw true beauty till this night.

· · · · · · · ·

ROMEO   If I profane with my unworthiest hand
         This holy shrine,[6] the gentle sin is this:
     My lips, two blushing pilgrims, ready stand
         To smooth that rough touch with a tender kiss.

JULIET   Good pilgrim, you do wrong your hand too much,
         Which mannerly devotion shows in this;
     For saints have hands that pilgrims' hands do touch,
         And palm to palm is holy palmers'[7] kiss.

ROMEO   Have not saints lips, and holy palmers too?

JULIET   Ay, pilgrim, lips that they must use in prayer.

ROMEO   O then, dear saint, let lips do what hands do:
         They pray; grant thou, lest faith turn to despair.

JULIET   Saints do not move, though grant for prayer's sake.[8]

ROMEO   Then move not while my prayer's effect I take.
     Thus from my lips, by thine, my sin is purged.
         [*He kisses her.*]

JULIET   Then have my lips the sin that they have took.

ROMEO   Sin from my lips? O trespass sweetly urged.
         Give me my sin again. [*He kisses her.*]

JULIET   You kiss by th'book.

Romeo escapes from his bawdy friends, and hides from them.
When they leave, he sees Juliet at her window (not a "balcony", as
is often supposed), and there follows the famous scene, captivating
in its portrayal of Romeo's extravagant romanticism and Juliet's

more pragmatic realism. Like new lovers everywhere, they find it unbearable to part, even for a few hours.

ACT 2, SCENES 1–2

BENVOLIO   Come, he hath hid himself among these trees
To be consorted with the humorous night.
Blind is his love, and best befits the dark.

MERCUTIO   If love be blind, love cannot hit the mark.
Now will he sit under a medlar[9] tree
And wish his mistress were that kind of fruit
As maids call medlars when they laugh alone.
O Romeo, that she were, O that she were
An open-arse[10] and thou a poperin[11] pear!
Romeo, good night. I'll to my truckle-bed;[12]
This field-bed[13] is too cold for me to sleep.
Come, shall we go?

BENVOLIO   Go then, for 'tis in vain
To seek him here that means not to be found.
                    Exeunt [*Benvolio and Mercutio*].

ROMEO   [*Comes forward.*] He jests at scars that never felt
            a wound.
            [*Enter Juliet above.*]
But soft, what light through yonder window breaks?
It is the East, and Juliet is the sun!
Arise, fair sun, and kill the envious moon,
Who is already sick and pale with grief
That thou her maid[14] art far more fair than she.
Be not her maid, since she is envious;
Her vestal livery[15] is but sick and green,
And none but fools do wear it. Cast it off.
It is my lady; O, it is my love!
O that she knew she were!

She speaks, yet she says nothing. What of that?

Her eye discourses; I will answer it.

I am too bold; 'tis not to me she speaks.

Two of the fairest stars in all the heaven,

Having some business, do entreat her eyes

To twinkle in their spheres[16] till they return.

What if her eyes were there, they in her head?

The brightness of her cheek would shame those stars

As daylight doth a lamp. Her eyes in heaven

Would through the airy region stream so bright

That birds would sing and think it were not night.

See how she leans her cheek upon her hand.

O that I were a glove upon that hand,

That I might touch that cheek.

JULIET   Ay me.

ROMEO   She speaks.

O speak again bright angel, for thou art

As glorious to this night, being o'er my head,

As is a winged messenger of heaven

Unto the white-upturned wondering eyes

Of mortals that fall back to gaze on him

When he bestrides the lazy-puffing clouds

And sails upon the bosom of the air.

JULIET   O Romeo, Romeo, wherefore art thou Romeo?[17]

Deny thy father and refuse thy name.

Or, if thou wilt not, be but sworn my love,

And I'll no longer be a Capulet.

ROMEO   [aside] Shall I hear more, or shall I speak at this?

JULIET   'Tis but thy name that is my enemy.

Thou art thyself, though not a Montague.

What's Montague? It is nor hand nor foot

Nor arm nor face, nor any other part

Belonging to a man. O, be some other name.
What's in a name? That which we call a rose
By any other word would smell as sweet;
So Romeo would, were he not Romeo called,
Retain that dear perfection which he owes
Without that title. Romeo, doff[18] thy name;
And for thy name, which is no part of thee,
Take all myself.

ROMEO   [*speaks aloud*] I take thee at thy word.
Call me but love, and I'll be new baptised:
Henceforth I never will be Romeo.

JULIET   What man art thou that, thus bescreened in night,
So stumblest on my counsel?

ROMEO   By a name
I know not how to tell thee who I am.
My name, dear saint, is hateful to myself
Because it is an enemy to thee.
Had I it written, I would tear the word.

JULIET   My ears have yet not drunk a hundred words
Of thy tongue's uttering, yet I know the sound.
Art thou not Romeo, and a Montague?

ROMEO   Neither, fair maid, if either thee dislike.

JULIET   How camest thou hither, tell me, and wherefore?
The orchard walls are high and hard to climb,
And the place death, considering who thou art,
If any of my kinsmen find thee here.

ROMEO   With love's light wings did I o'erperch[19] these walls,
For stony limits cannot hold love out,
And what love can do, that dares love attempt.
Therefore thy kinsmen are no stop to me.

JULIET   If they do see thee, they will murder thee.

ROMEO   Alack, there lies more peril in thine eye

	Than twenty of their swords. Look thou but sweet,
	And I am proof against their enmity.
JULIET	I would not for the world they saw thee here.
ROMEO	I have night's cloak to hide me from their eyes,
	And but thou love me, let them find me here.
	My life were better ended by their hate
	Than death proroguèd,[20] wanting of thy love.
JULIET	By whose direction found'st thou out this place?
ROMEO	By love, that first did prompt me to enquire.
	He lent me counsel, and I lent him eyes.
	I am no pilot, yet wert thou as far
	As that vast shore washed with the farthest sea,
	I should adventure for such merchandise.
JULIET	Thou knowest the mask of night is on my face,
	Else would a maiden blush bepaint my cheek
	For that which thou hast heard me speak tonight.
	Fain would I dwell on form—fain, fain deny
	What I have spoke; but farewell compliment.[21]
	Dost thou love me? I know thou wilt say "Ay",
	And I will take thy word. Yet, if thou swear'st,
	Thou mayst prove false. At lovers' perjuries,
	They say, Jove[22] laughs. O gentle Romeo,
	If thou dost love, pronounce it faithfully.
	Or, if thou think'st I am too quickly won,
	I'll frown and be perverse, and say thee nay,
	So thou wilt woo; but else, not for the world.
	In truth, fair Montague, I am too fond,[23]
	And therefore thou mayst think my 'haviour light;[24]
	But trust me, gentleman, I'll prove more true
	Than those that have more cunning to be strange.[25]
	I should have been more strange, I must confess,
	But that thou overheard'st, ere I was ware,

	My true-love passion; therefore pardon me,

My true-love passion; therefore pardon me,

And not impute this yielding to light love,

Which the dark night hath so discovered.

ROMEO   Lady, by yonder blessed moon I vow,

That tips with silver all these fruit-tree tops—

JULIET   O swear not by the moon, th'inconstant moon,

That monthly changes in her circled orb,

Lest that thy love prove likewise variable.

ROMEO   What shall I swear by?

JULIET   　　　　　　　　　Do not swear at all.

Or if thou wilt, swear by thy gracious self,

Which is the god of my idolatry,

And I'll believe thee.

ROMEO   　　　　　　　　If my heart's dear love—

JULIET   Well, do not swear. Although I joy in thee,

I have no joy of this contract tonight.

It is too rash, too unadvised, too sudden;

Too like the lightning, which doth cease to be

Ere one can say "It lightens." Sweet, good night.

This bud of love, by summer's ripening breath,

May prove a beauteous flower when next we meet.

Good night, good night. As sweet repose and rest

Come to thy heart as that within my breast.

ROMEO   O, wilt thou leave me so unsatisfied?

JULIET   What satisfaction canst thou have tonight?

ROMEO   Th'exchange of thy love's faithful vow for mine.

JULIET   I gave thee mine before thou didst request it;

And yet I would it were to give again.

ROMEO   Wouldst thou withdraw it? For what purpose, love?

JULIET   But to be frank and give it thee again.

And yet I wish but for the thing I have.

My bounty is as boundless as the sea,

	My love as deep; the more I give to thee
	The more I have, for both are infinite.
	I hear some noise within. Dear love, adieu.
	[*Nurse calls within.*]
	Anon, good nurse—Sweet Montague be true.
	Stay but a little, I will come again. [*Exit Juliet.*]
ROMEO	O blessèd, blessèd night. I am afeard,
	Being in night, all this is but a dream,
	Too flattering-sweet to be substantial.
	[*Re-enter Juliet above.*]
JULIET	Three words, dear Romeo, and good night indeed.
	If that thy bent[26] of love be honourable,
	Thy purpose marriage, send me word tomorrow,
	By one that I'll procure to come to thee,
	Where and what time thou wilt perform the rite,
	And all my fortunes at thy foot I'll lay,
	And follow thee my lord throughout the world.
NURSE	[*within*] Madam!
JULIET	I come, anon—But if thou meanest not well,
	I do beseech thee—
NURSE	[*within*] Madam!
JULIET	By and by I come—
	To cease thy strife and leave me to my grief.
	Tomorrow will I send.
ROMEO	So thrive my soul—
JULIET	A thousand times good night. [*Exit Juliet.*]
ROMEO	A thousand times the worse, to want thy light.
	Love goes toward love as schoolboys from their books,
	But love from love, toward school with heavy looks.
	Enter Juliet [*above*] *again.*
JULIET	Hist! Romeo, hist! O for a falconer's voice

To lure this tercel-gentle[27] back again.
Bondage is hoarse and may not speak aloud,
Else would I tear the cave where Echo lies,
And make her airy tongue more hoarse than mine
With repetition of "my Romeo".

ROMEO It is my soul that calls upon my name.
How silver-sweet sound lovers' tongues by night,
Like softest music to attending ears.

JULIET Romeo.

ROMEO My dear?

JULIET What o'clock tomorrow
Shall I send to thee?

ROMEO By the hour of nine.

JULIET I will not fail. 'Tis twenty year till then.
I have forgot why I did call thee back.

ROMEO Let me stand here till thou remember it.

JULIET I shall forget, to have thee still stand there,
Remembering how I love thy company.

ROMEO And I'll still stay to have thee still forget,
Forgetting any other home but this.

JULIET 'Tis almost morning. I would have thee gone—
And yet no farther than a wanton's[28] bird,
That lets it hop a little from his hand,
Like a poor prisoner in his twisted gyves,[29]
And with a silken thread plucks it back again,
So loving-jealous of his liberty.

ROMEO I would I were thy bird.

JULIET Sweet, so would I.
Yet I should kill thee with much cherishing.
Good night, good night. Parting is such sweet sorrow
That I shall say good night till it be morrow.
    [*Exit Juliet.*]

ROMEO	Sleep dwell upon thine eyes, peace in thy breast.
	Would I were sleep and peace so sweet to rest.
	Hence will I to my ghostly Friar's close cell,
	His help to crave and my dear hap to tell. *Exit.*

The lyrical mood of the play ends abruptly when Romeo kills Juliet's cousin Tybalt in a duel. Juliet, unaware of the tragic turn the action has taken, anticipates Romeo's arrival in a soliloquy, where her naïve eroticism is the more deeply affecting because of our awareness that her happy fantasy is about to be shattered by the events we have just seen on stage.

ACT 3, SCENE 1

JULIET	Gallop apace, you fiery-footed steeds,
	Towards Phoebus'[30] lodging. Such a wagonner
	As Phaeton[31] would whip you to the West
	And bring in cloudy night immediately.
	Spread thy close curtain, love-performing night,
	That runaway's eyes may wink,[32] and Romeo
	Leap to these arms untalked-of and unseen.
	Lovers can see to do their amorous rites
	By their own beauties; or, if love be blind,
	It best agrees with night. Come, civil night,
	Thou sober-suited matron, all in black,
	And learn[33] me how to lose a winning match
	Played for a pair of stainless maidenhoods.
	Hood my unmanned blood, bating[34] in my cheeks,
	With thy black mantle, till strange love grow bold,
	Think true love acted simple modesty.
	Come night, come Romeo, come, thou day in night,
	For thou wilt lie upon the wings of night
	Whiter than new snow upon a raven's back.

Come gentle night, come loving, black-browed
    night,
Give me my Romeo; and when he shall die
Take him and cut him out in little stars,
And he will make the face of heaven so fine
That all the world will be in love with night,
And pay no worship to the garish sun.
O, I have bought the mansion of a love
But not possessed it, and though I am sold,
Not yet enjoyed. So tedious is this day
As is the night before some festival
To an impatient child that hath new robes
And may not wear them.

After their one night together, Romeo must leave for Mantua, the city of his banishment, or face death for disobeying the Prince. He has, of necessity, matured, as he is deeply aware of the consequences of remaining.

ACT 3, SCENE 5

        Enter Romeo and Juliet aloft at the window.

JULIET   Wilt thou be gone? It is not yet near day.
        It was the nightingale and not the lark
        That pierced the fearful hollow of thine ear.
        Nightly she sings on yond pomegranate tree.
        Believe me, love, it was the nightingale.
ROMEO   It was the lark, the herald of the morn,
        No nightingale. Look, love, what envious streaks
        Do lace the severing clouds in yonder East.
        Night's candles are burnt out, and jocund[35] day
        Stands tiptoe on the misty mountain tops.
        I must be gone and live, or stay and die.

JULIET	Yond light is not daylight, I know it, I.
	It is some meteor that the sun exhales
	To be to thee this night a torchbearer
	And light thee on thy way to Mantua.
	Therefore stay yet; thou need'st not to be gone.
ROMEO	Let me be ta'en, let me be put to death,
	I am content, so thou wilt have it so. . . .
	I have more care to stay than will to go.
	Come death, and welcome. Juliet wills it so.
	How is't, my soul? Let's talk; it is not day.
JULIET	It is, it is. Hie hence, begone, away!
	It is the lark that sings so out of tune,
	Straining harsh discords and unpleasing sharps.[36]
	Some say the lark makes sweet division;[37]
	This doth not so, for she divideth us. . . .
	O, now be gone, more light and light it grows.
ROMEO	More light and light—more dark and dark our woes.

In the last scene, Romeo, believing Juliet to be truly dead, returns to Verona. At the door to the Capulets' tomb, he finds his rival, Paris, in his way. He kills Paris and forces his way into the tomb. In another stroke of bad luck, the friar arrives too late to stop him from taking the poison he has acquired from an apothecary. Some modern performances omit the friar from this scene, allowing Juliet to awaken as Romeo dies.

ACT 5, SCENE 3

ROMEO	Here lies Juliet, and her beauty makes
	This vault a feasting presence, full of light.
	Death, lie thou there, by a dead man interred.
	[Lays Paris beside Juliet.]
	How oft when men are at the point of death

Have they been merry!— which their keepers call
A lightning before death. O, how may I
Call this a lightning? O my love, my wife,
Death, that hath sucked the honey of thy breath,
Hath had no power yet upon thy beauty.
Thou art not conquered. Beauty's ensign[38] yet
Is crimson in thy lips and in thy cheeks,
And Death's pale flag is not advancèd there.
Tybalt, liest thou there in thy bloody sheet?
O, what more favour can I do to thee
Than with that hand that cut thy youth in twain
To sunder his that was thine enemy?
Forgive me, cousin. Ah, dear Juliet,
Why art thou yet so fair? Shall I believe
That unsubstantial Death is amorous,
And that the lean abhorrèd monster keeps
Thee here in dark to be his paramour?

For fear of that I still[39] will stay with thee,

And never from this palace of dim night

Depart again. Here, here will I remain

With worms that are thy chambermaids. O here

Will I set up my everlasting rest

And shake the yoke of inauspicious stars[40]

From this world-wearied flesh. Eyes, look your last.

Arms, take your last embrace, and lips, O you,

The doors of breath, seal with a righteous kiss

A dateless bargain to engrossing Death.

Come, bitter conduct;[41] come, unsavoury guide;

Thou desperate pilot, now at once run on

The dashing rocks thy seasick weary bark.[42]

Here's to my love! [*He drinks.*] O true apothecary,

Thy drugs are quick. Thus with a kiss I die. [*He falls.*]

> Enter Friar [Laurence], with lantern, crow[bar],
>
> and spade.

FRIAR   Saint Francis be my speed! How oft tonight

Have my old feet stumbled at graves.

Friar stoops and looks on the blood and weapons.

Romeo! O, pale! Who else? What, Paris too?

And steeped in blood? Ah, what an unkind hour

Is guilty of this lamentable chance!

The lady stirs. [*Juliet wakes.*]

JULIET   O comfortable Friar, where is my lord?

I do remember well where I should be,

And there I am. Where is my Romeo?

> [*a noise within*]

FRIAR   I hear some noise. Lady, come from that nest

Of death, contagion, and unnatural sleep.

A greater power than we can contradict

Hath thwarted our intents. Come, come away.

	Thy husband in thy bosom there lies dead,
	And Paris too. Come, I'll dispose of thee
	Among a sisterhood of holy nuns.
	Stay not to question, for the Watch[43] is coming.
	Come, go, good Juliet. I dare no longer stay.
JULIET	Go, get thee hence, for I will not away. *Exit [Friar].*
	What's here? A cup, closed in my true love's hand?
	Poison, I see, hath been his timeless[44] end.
	O churl, drunk all, and left no friendly drop
	To help me after? I will kiss thy lips.
	Haply some poison yet doth hang on them
	To make me die with a restorative. [*She kisses him.*]
	Thy lips are warm!
WATCH	[*within*] Lead, boy. Which way?
JULIET	Yea, noise? Then I'll be brief. O happy dagger,
	[*She takes Romeo's dagger.*]
	This is thy sheath; there rest, and let me die.
	[*She stabs herself and dies.*]

. . . .

PRINCE	A glooming peace this morning with it brings.
	The sun for sorrow will not show his head.
	Go hence to have more talk of these sad things.
	Some shall be pardoned, and some punishèd;
	For never was a story of more woe
	Than this of Juliet and her Romeo.

The Merchant of Venice

Shakespeare's early works highlight the difficulties faced by young lovers in both tragic and comic circumstances. Three great comedies of his maturity, however, offer somewhat more optimistic outcomes, though this optimism is somewhat qualified by the titles he gave the plays, all of which suggest an awareness that happy endings in love are more the result of audience demand than the real world: *As You Like It*, *Much Ado About Nothing* and *Twelfth Night, Or What You Will*.

In each of these comedies there is a continuing anxiety about the transience of love and the difficulty of keeping the spark alive. The best-matched lovers in Shakespeare's works, Rosalind and Orlando in *As You Like It*, and Beatrice and Benedick in *Much Ado About Nothing*, persuade us to believe in the genuineness of their love because of their willingness to challenge each other. Rosalind proclaims that wise lovers (especially the women, if they want to keep their men) must be "wayward", or changeable; Benedick, after yet another sparring match with Beatrice, comments that they are "too wise to woo peaceably".

Perhaps harmonious love is impossible to achieve; even in the early sonnets, the youth listens with sadness to "the true concord of well-tunèd sounds" (sonnet 8). Music and love are also closely associated in the plays, as the next two selections show. After the high drama of the troubling court scene where Shylock is defeated and forced to convert to Christianity, Shakespeare brings the mood of *The Merchant of Venice* to a more comic close in the final scene. Jessica, Shylock's daughter, and her new husband, Lorenzo, await the arrival of the main characters in the moonlight. The scene begins with what might be a gentle competition – or an episode of marital bickering. The two remind each other of a series of famous, but ill-fated lovers; the potential conflict is resolved, at least for the time being, by music.

ACT 5, SCENE 1

Enter Lorenzo and Jessica.

LORENZO   The moon shines bright. In such a night as this,
When the sweet wind did gently kiss the trees,
And they did make no noise, in such a night
Troilus methinks mounted the Trojan walls,
And sighed his soul toward the Grecian tents
Where Cressid lay that night.[1]

JESSICA   In such a night
Did Thisbe[2] fearfully o'ertrip the dew,
And saw the lion's shadow ere himself,
And ran dismayed away.

LORENZO   In such a night
Stood Dido[3] with a willow[4] in her hand
Upon the wild sea banks, and waft her love
To come again to Carthage.

JESSICA   In such a night
Medea[5] gathered the enchanted herbs
That did renew old Aeson.

LORENZO   In such a night
Did Jessica steal from the wealthy Jew,
And with an unthrift love did run from Venice,
As far as Belmont.[6]

JESSICA   In such a night
Did young Lorenzo swear he loved her well,
Stealing her soul with many vows of faith,
And ne'er a true one.

LORENZO   In such a night
Did pretty Jessica, like a little shrew,
Slander her love, and he forgave it her.

       . . . .

How sweet the moonlight sleeps upon this bank!

Here will we sit, and let the sounds of music
Creep in our ears. Soft stillness and the night
Become[7] the touches of sweet harmony.
Sit, Jessica. Look how the floor of heaven
Is thick inlaid with patens[8] of bright gold.
There's not the smallest orb which thou behold'st
But in his motion like an angel sings,
Still choiring to the young-eyed cherubins;
Such harmony is in immortal souls,
But whilst this muddy vesture of decay[9]
Doth grossly close it in, we cannot hear it.

    [*Enter Musicians.*]

Come, ho, and wake Diana[10] with a hymn!
With sweetest touches pierce your mistress' ear
And draw her home with music.   *music*

JESSICA   I am never merry when I hear sweet music.

LORENZO   The reason is your spirits are attentive.
For do but note a wild and wanton herd,
Or race[11] of youthful and unhandled colts . . .
If they but hear perchance a trumpet sound,
Or any air of music touch their ears,
You shall perceive them make a mutual stand,
Their savage eyes turned to a modest gaze
By the sweet power of music. . . .
The man that hath no music in himself,
Nor is not moved with concord of sweet sounds,
Is fit for treasons, stratagems, and spoils;
The motions of his spirit are dull as night
And his affections dark as Erebus.[12]
Let no such man be trusted. Mark the music.

Twelfth Night

If *The Merchant of Venice* ends with harmony, *Twelfth Night* opens with a famous passage on love and music. Orsino dismisses music in his irritation at facing an unrequited passion; the passage as a whole suggests that he is both impatient and sceptical of the ultimate value of love. It is fitting, therefore, that in the play he undergoes a trial where he discovers that friendship is an essential pre-condition to love; only at the end does he discover love for the wit and integrity of Viola, whom he has befriended in her disguise as a young man.

ACT 1, SCENE 1

ORSINO   If music be the food of love, play on,
Give me excess of it, that, surfeiting,[1]
The appetite may sicken, and so die.
That strain[2] again! It had a dying fall;
O, it came o'er my ear like the sweet sound
That breathes upon a bank of violets,
Stealing and giving odour. Enough, no more;
'Tis not so sweet now as it was before.
O spirit of love, how quick and fresh art thou,
That notwithstanding thy capacity
Receiveth as the sea, nought enters there,
Of what validity and pitch soe'er,
But falls into abatement and low price,[3]
Even in a minute! So full of shapes is fancy,[4]
That it alone is high fantastical.[5]

As You Like It

In another gender-bending comedy, Rosalind disguises herself as a young man to escape from her cruel uncle; she and her cousin Celia flee to the Forest of Arden, where she discovers that her new love, Orlando, has also been banished to the forest, and has been papering the trees with hyperbolic (and rather bad) poems addressed to her. In her masculine disguise, she is able to propose a "cure" to Orlando; in the process she is able to find out whether his love is genuine, and whether they can be friends as well as lovers. Shakespeare enjoys the irony where Rosalind cheerfully lists the "giddy offences" laid at the door of women in general.

ACT 3, SCENE 2

ORLANDO   Where dwell you pretty youth?

ROSALIND   With this shepherdess, my sister;[1] here in the skirts of the forest, like fringe upon a petticoat.

ORLANDO   Are you native of this place?

ROSALIND   As the coney[2] that you see dwell where she is kindled.[3]

ORLANDO   Your accent is something finer than you could purchase in so removed a dwelling.

ROSALIND   I have been told so of many. But indeed, an old religious uncle of mine taught me to speak, who was in his youth an inland man;[4] one that knew courtship too well, for there he fell in love. I have heard him read many lectures against it, and I thank God I am not a woman, to be touched with so many giddy offences as he hath generally taxed their whole sex withal.

ORLANDO   Can you remember any of the principal evils that he laid to the charge of women?

ROSALIND	There were none principal; they were all like one another as halfpence are, every one fault seeming monstrous till his fellow-fault came to match it.
ORLANDO	I prithee recount some of them.
ROSALIND	No; I will not cast away my physic[5] but on those that are sick. There is a man haunts the forest that abuses our young plants with carving "Rosalind" on their barks; hangs odes upon hawthorns and elegies on brambles; all, forsooth, deifying the name of Rosalind. If I could meet that fancy-monger,[6] I would give him some good counsel, for he seems to have the quotidian[7] of love upon him.
ORLANDO	I am he that is so love-shaked; I pray you tell me your remedy.
ROSALIND	There is none of my uncle's marks upon you. He taught me how to know a man in love; in which cage of rushes[8] I am sure you are not prisoner.
ORLANDO	What were his marks?
ROSALIND	A lean cheek, which you have not; a blue eye and sunken, which you have not; an unquestionable spirit, which you have not; a beard neglected, which you have not—but I pardon you for that, for simply your having in beard is a younger brother's revenue.[9] Then your hose should be ungartered, your bonnet unbanded, your sleeve unbuttoned, your shoe untied, and everything about you demonstrating a careless desolation.[10] But you are no such man: you are rather point-device[11] in your accoutrements,[12] as loving yourself than seeming the lover of any other.
ORLANDO	Fair youth, I would I could make thee believe I love.
ROSALIND	Me believe it! You may as soon make her that you

love believe it, which I warrant she is apter to do than to confess she does. That is one of the points in the which women still give the lie to their consciences. But, in good sooth,[13] are you he that hangs the verses on the trees wherein Rosalind is so admired?

ORLANDO   I swear to thee, youth, by the white hand of Rosalind, I am that he, that unfortunate he.

ROSALIND   But are you so much in love as your rhymes speak?

ORLANDO   Neither rhyme nor reason can express how much.

ROSALIND   Love is merely a madness, and I tell you, deserves as well a dark house and a whip as madmen do;[14] and the reason why they are not so punished and cured is that the lunacy is so ordinary that the whippers are in love too. Yet I profess curing it by counsel.

ORLANDO   Did you ever cure any so?

ROSALIND   Yes, one, and in this manner. He was to imagine me his love, his mistress; and I set him every day to woo me. At which time would I, being but a moonish[15] youth, grieve, be effeminate, changeable, longing and liking,

proud, fantastical, apish, shallow, inconstant, full of tears, full of smiles, for every passion something and for no passion truly anything, as boys and women are for the most part cattle of this colour; would now like him, now loathe him; then entertain him, then forswear him; now weep for him, then spit at him; that I drove my suitor from his mad humour of love to a living humour of madness,[16] which was, to forswear the full stream of the world and to live in a nook merely monastic. And thus I cured him; and this way will I take upon me to wash your liver[17] as clean as a sound sheep's heart, that there shall not be one spot of love in't.

ORLANDO   I would not be cured, youth.

ROSALIND   I would cure you, if you would but call me Rosalind and come every day to my cote[18] and woo me.

ORLANDO   Now by the faith of my love, I will.

Rosalind (disguised as the youth "Ganymede") continues her game of pretending to be herself. She puts into practice her belief that if it is to survive, love must be forever changing, forever challenging; and in the face of Orlando's romantic idealism she provides a dose of reality, again using examples from Greek myth.

ACT 4, SCENE 1

ROSALIND   Come, woo me, woo me; for now I am in a holiday humour and like enough to consent. What would you say to me now, an I were your very very[19] Rosalind?

ORLANDO   I would kiss before I spoke.

ROSALIND   Nay, you were better speak first, and when you were gravelled[20] for lack of matter, you might take occasion to kiss. Very good orators, when they are out,[21] they

will spit; and for lovers lacking—God warrant us!—
matter, the cleanliest shift is to kiss.

ORLANDO   How if the kiss be denied?

ROSALIND   Then she puts you to entreaty, and there begins new
matter.

ORLANDO   Who could be out, being before his beloved mistress?

ROSALIND   Marry, that should you, if I were your mistress, or I
should think my honesty ranker[22] than my wit.

ORLANDO   What, of my suit?

ROSALIND   Not out of your apparel, and yet out of your suit.[23]
Am not I your Rosalind?

ORLANDO   I take some joy to say you are, because I would be
talking of her.

ROSALIND   Well, in her person, I say I will not have you.

ORLANDO   Then in mine own person, I die.

ROSALIND   No, faith, die by attorney.[24] The poor world is
almost six thousand years old,[25] and in all this time
there was not any man died in his own person,
videlicet,[26] in a love-cause. Troilus had his brains
dashed out with a Grecian club, yet he did what he
could to die before, and he is one of the patterns of
love. Leander, he would have lived many a fair year
though Hero[27] had turned nun, if it had not been
for a hot midsummer night; for, good youth, he
went but forth to wash him in the Hellespont and
being taken with the cramp, was drowned; and
the foolish chroniclers of that age found it was—Hero
of Sestos. But these are all lies. Men have died from
time to time, and worms have eaten them, but not
for love.

ORLANDO   I would not have my right Rosalind of this mind; for,
I protest, her frown might kill me.

ROSALIND	By this hand, it will not kill a fly. But come, now I will be your Rosalind in a more coming-on disposition; and ask me what you will, I will grant it.
ORLANDO	Then love me Rosalind.
ROSALIND	Yes, faith, will I, Fridays and Saturdays and all.
ORLANDO	And wilt thou have me?
ROSALIND	Ay, and twenty such.
ORLANDO	What sayest thou?
ROSALIND	Are you not good?
ORLANDO	I hope so.
ROSALIND	Why then, can one desire too much of a good thing? Come sister, you shall be the priest and marry us. Give me your hand, Orlando. What do you say, sister?
ORLANDO	Pray thee, marry us.
CELIA	I cannot say the words.
ROSALIND	You must begin, "Will you, Orlando"—
CELIA	Go to. Will you, Orlando, have to wife this Rosalind?
ORLANDO	I will.
ROSALIND	Ay, but when?
ORLANDO	Why now, as fast as she can marry us.
ROSALIND	Then you must say "I take thee, Rosalind, for wife."
ORLANDO	I take thee, Rosalind, for wife.
ROSALIND	I might ask you for your commission;[28] but I do take thee, Orlando, for my husband. There's a girl goes before the priest, and certainly a woman's thought runs before her actions.
ORLANDO	So do all thoughts; they are winged.
ROSALIND	Now tell me how long you would have her, after you have possessed her.
ORLANDO	For ever and a day.
ROSALIND	Say "a day" without the "ever". No, no, Orlando, men are April when they woo, December when they wed.

Maids are May when they are maids, but the sky changes when they are wives. I will be more jealous of thee than a Barbary cock-pigeon over his hen, more clamorous than a parrot against rain, more new-fangled[29] than an ape, more giddy in my desires than a monkey. I will weep for nothing, like Diana in the fountain,[30] and I will do that when you are disposed to be merry; I will laugh like a hyena, and that when thou art inclined to sleep.

ORLANDO   But will my Rosalind do so?

ROSALIND   By my life, she will do as I do.

ORLANDO   Oh, but she is wise.

ROSALIND   Or else she could not have the wit to do this. The wiser, the waywarder. Make the doors upon a woman's wit, and it will out at the casement; shut that, and 'twill out at the keyhole; stop that, 'twill fly with the smoke out at the chimney.

In these brief selections, it is impossible to give a sense of the breadth of Shakespeare's exploration of the nature of love in *As You Like It*. There are, in fact, four couples of various ranks and personalities involved, and one of these pairings is complicated by the fact that Silvius's female partner, Phebe, has fallen in love with Rosalind in her disguise as the youth Ganymede. At the climax of the play, Rosalind takes command, promising to bring them all together.

ACT 5, SCENE 2

PHEBE	Good shepherd, tell this youth what 'tis to love.
SILVIUS	It is to be all made of sighs and tears;
	And so am I for Phebe.
PHEBE	And I for Ganymede.
ORLANDO	And I for Rosalind.
ROSALIND	And I for no woman.
SILVIUS	It is to be all made of faith and service;
	And so am I for Phebe.
PHEBE	And I for Ganymede.
ORLANDO	And I for Rosalind.
ROSALIND	And I for no woman.
SILVIUS	It is to be all made of fantasy,
	All made of passion, and all made of wishes,
	All adoration, duty, and observance,
	All humbleness, all patience, and impatience,
	All purity, all trial, all observance;
	And so am I for Phebe.
PHEBE	And so am I for Ganymede.
ORLANDO	And so am I for Rosalind.
ROSALIND	And so am I for no woman.
PHEBE	[*to Rosalind*] If this be so, why blame you me to love you?
SILVIUS	[*to Phebe*] If this be so, why blame you me to love you?
ORLANDO	If this be so, why blame you me to love you?
ROSALIND	Why do you speak too, "Why blame you me to love you?"
ORLANDO	To her that is not here, nor doth not hear.
ROSALIND	Pray you no more of this; 'tis like the howling of Irish wolves against the moon.

Much Ado About Nothing

In this play there are two pairs of lovers, one naïve, the other experienced. Young Claudio falls in love with Hero, but scarcely knows her, and is easily deceived by the melancholy Don John into thinking she has been false to him. Beatrice and Benedick, on the other hand, are older, and have been attracted to each other in the past – but Benedick shied away from commitment. Now when they meet there is a "merry war" of wits between them. Their friends decide to trick them into admitting their love for each other: each is to overhear their friends discussing how the other is madly in love but too proud to admit it.

Shakespeare repeats the abrupt changes in love that he plotted in *A Midsummer Night's Dream*, but this time it is human psychology, not a magic potion, that causes the changes. In this first passage, Benedick has just heard that Beatrice is (supposedly) deeply in love with him. It is as if he had been given permission to admit his own love, and he immediately finds all kinds of good reasons why he should indeed be in love with her. When Beatrice enters, however, she has not yet been converted – though he is convinced he sees her love for him. Once again, Shakespeare heightens comedy through irony.

ACT 2, SCENE 3

[*Benedick advances from the arbour.*]

BENEDICK   This can be no trick. The conference was sadly[1] borne; they have the truth of this from Hero. They seem to pity the lady. It seems her affections have their full bent. Love me? Why, it must be requited. I hear how I am censured. They say I will bear myself proudly if I perceive the love come from her. They say too that she will rather die than give any sign of affection. I did never think to marry. I must not seem proud. Happy are they that hear their detractions and can put them to mending. They say the lady is fair—'tis a truth, I can bear them witness; and virtuous—'tis so, I cannot reprove it; and wise, but for loving me. By my troth, it is no addition to her wit—nor no great argument of her folly, for I will be horribly in love with her. I may chance have some odd quirks² and remnants of wit broken on me because I have railed so long against marriage. But doth not the appetite alter? A man loves the meat in his youth that he cannot endure in his age. Shall quips and sentences and these paper bullets of the brain³ awe a man from the career of his humour?⁴ No, the world must be peopled. When I said I would die a bachelor, I did not think I should live till I were married.

    Enter Beatrice.

Here comes Beatrice. By this day, she's a fair lady! I do spy some marks of love in her.

BEATRICE	Against my will I am sent to bid you come in to dinner.
BENEDICK	Fair Beatrice, I thank you for your pains.
BEATRICE	I took no more pains for those thanks than you take pains to thank me. If it had been painful, I would not have come.
BENEDICK	You take pleasure then in the message?
BEATRICE	Yea, just so much as you may take upon a knife's point and choke a daw⁵ withal. You have no stomach,⁶ signior. Fare you well. *Exit.*
BENEDICK	Ha! "Against my will I am sent to bid you come in to dinner." There's a double meaning in that. "I took no

more pains for those thanks than you took pains to thank me." That's as much as to say, "Any pains that I take for you is as easy as thanks." If I do not take pity of her, I am a villain; if I do not love her, I am a Jew. I will go get her picture.   *Exit.*

Beatrice and Benedick admit their love for each other in an extraordinary scene. Claudio, deceived by the villainous Don John into believing that Hero has been unfaithful to him, has just denounced Hero at the altar where he was supposed to have married her. She has fainted, and Claudio has left. Benedick remains behind; the friar who was to have performed the marriage suggests that they announce that Hero has died rather than merely fainted. Benedick is left alone with Beatrice. The scene is deeply complicated by Beatrice's fury at the treatment her friend has received.

ACT 4, SCENE 1

BENEDICK	Lady Beatrice, have you wept all this while?
BEATRICE	Yea, and I will weep a while longer.
BENEDICK	I will not desire that.
BEATRICE	You have no reason, I do it freely.
BENEDICK	Surely I do believe your fair cousin is wronged.
BEATRICE	Ah, how much might the man deserve of me that would right her!
BENEDICK	Is there any way to show such friendship?
BEATRICE	A very even way, but no such friend.
BENEDICK	May a man do it?
BEATRICE	It is a man's office, but not yours.
BENEDICK	I do love nothing in the world so well as you. Is not that strange?
BEATRICE	As strange as the thing I know not. It were as possible for me to say I loved nothing so well as you. But

believe me not; and yet I lie not. I confess nothing, nor I deny nothing. I am sorry for my cousin.

BENEDICK By my sword, Beatrice, thou lovest me.

BEATRICE Do not swear, and eat it.

BENEDICK I will swear by it that you love me, and I will make him eat it that says I love not you.

BEATRICE Will you not eat your word?

BENEDICK With no sauce that can be devised to it. I protest I love thee.

BEATRICE Why then, God forgive me!

BENEDICK What offence, sweet Beatrice?

BEATRICE You have stayed me in a happy hour.[7] I was about to protest I loved you.

BENEDICK And do it with all thy heart.

BEATRICE I love you with so much of my heart that none is left to protest.

BENEDICK Come, bid me do anything for thee.

BEATRICE Kill Claudio.

BENEDICK Ha, not for the wide world!

BEATRICE You kill me to deny it. Farewell.

BENEDICK Tarry, sweet Beatrice. [*He holds her.*]

BEATRICE I am gone, though I am here. There is no love in you. Nay, I pray you let me go.

BENEDICK Beatrice—

BEATRICE In faith, I will go.

BENEDICK We'll be friends first. [*He releases her.*]

BEATRICE You dare easier be friends with me than fight with mine enemy.

BENEDICK Is Claudio thine enemy?

BEATRICE Is he not approved[8] in the height a villain, that hath slandered, scorned, dishonoured my kinswoman? Oh that I were a man! What? bear her in hand[9] until they

	come to take hands, and then with public accusation, uncovered slander, unmitigated rancour—O God, that I were a man! I would eat his heart in the market place.
BENEDICK	Hear me, Beatrice!
BEATRICE	Talk with a man out at a window! A proper saying!
BENEDICK	Nay but Beatrice—
BEATRICE	Sweet Hero! she is wronged, she is slandered, she is undone.
BENEDICK	Beat—
BEATRICE	Princes and Counties![10] Surely a princely testimony, a goodly count, Count Comfect,[11] a sweet gallant surely! Oh that I were a man for his[12] sake! or that I had any friend would be a man for my sake! But manhood is melted into cursties, valour into compliment, and men are only turned into tongue,[13] and trim ones too. He is now as valiant as Hercules that only tells a lie and swears it. I cannot be a man with wishing; therefore I will die a woman with grieving.
BENEDICK	Tarry, good Beatrice. By this hand I love thee.
BEATRICE	Use it for my love some other way than swearing by it.
BENEDICK	Think you in your soul the Count Claudio hath wronged Hero?
BEATRICE	Yea, as sure as I have a thought or a soul.
BENEDICK	Enough. I am engaged.[14] I will challenge him. I will kiss your hand, and so I leave you. By this hand, Claudio shall render me a dear account.[15] As you hear of me, so think of me. Go comfort your cousin. I must say she is dead—and so farewell.

Benedick is as good as his word in this last speech, and he challenges Claudio to a duel. As he awaits Claudio's response, Benedick struggles to play the part of the traditional lover; Shakespeare reminds us again of the unfortunate loves of Greek myth, as Benedick attempts to suppress his ironic view of the world in order to write a love poem to Beatrice.

ACT 5, SCENE 2

MARGARET   Well, I will call Beatrice to you, who I think hath legs.

BENEDICK   And therefore will come.   *Exit Margaret.*

[*Sings*] The god of love,

> That sits above,
>
> And knows me, and knows me,
>
> How pitiful I deserve—

I mean in singing; but in loving, Leander the good swimmer, Troilus the first employer of panders,[16] and a whole bookful of these quondam carpet-mongers,[17] whose names yet run smoothly in the even road of a blank verse, why, they were never so truly turned over and over as my poor self in love. Marry, I cannot show it in rhyme. I have tried. I can find out no rhyme to "lady" but "baby"—an innocent rhyme; for "scorn", "horn"—a hard rhyme; for "school", "fool"— a babbling rhyme: very ominous endings! No, I was not born under a rhyming planet, nor I cannot woo in festival terms.

> *Enter Beatrice.*

Sweet Beatrice, wouldst thou come when I called thee?

BEATRICE   Yea, signior, and depart when you bid me.

BENEDICK   O, stay but till then!

BEATRICE   "Then" is spoken; fare you well now. And yet, ere I go, let me go with that I came, which is, with knowing what hath passed between you and Claudio.

BENEDICK	Only foul words; and thereupon I will kiss thee.
BEATRICE	Foul words is but foul wind, and foul wind is but foul breath, and foul breath is noisome; therefore I will depart unkissed.
BENEDICK	Thou hast frighted the word out of his right sense, so forcible is thy wit. But I must tell thee plainly, Claudio undergoes my challenge, and either I must shortly hear from him, or I will subscribe[18] him a coward. And I pray thee now tell me, for which of my bad parts didst thou first fall in love with me?
BEATRICE	For them all together, which maintained so politic a state of evil that they will not admit any good part to intermingle with them. But for which of my good parts did you first suffer love for me?
BENEDICK	Suffer love!—a good epithet. I do suffer love indeed, for I love thee against my will.
BEATRICE	In spite of your heart, I think. Alas, poor heart! If you spite it for my sake, I will spite it for yours, for I will never love that which my friend hates.
BENEDICK	Thou and I are too wise to woo peaceably.

At the close of this scene, the plot of Don John comes to light, and in due course the younger couple reunite; the play ends with two marriages, as Benedick calls for a festive dance "to lighten our hearts and our wives' heels".

3

NOT WISELY, BUT TOO WELL

Richard III

Much of the drama of Shakespeare's great comedies comes from the moments of tension and challenge in love; no love is ever simple to attain or to sustain. In this chapter there are selections from a group of plays that unflinchingly explore the darker side of love: envy, selfish sexual desire and jealousy. The plays in this section range from an early history, *Richard III*, to *Othello*, a tragedy of love written at the height of Shakespeare's career.

In his early historical tragedy of blood and power *Richard III*, Shakespeare provides a Machiavellian counterpoint to the breathtakingly romantic wooing scene in *Romeo and Juliet*. Many members of Shakespeare's audience would have seen the earlier histories of *Henry VI*, where Richard, Duke of Gloucester, begins his ruthless ascent to the throne. Shakespeare depicts Richard as a "hunchback", deeply conscious of his deformity.[1] In the opening speech of the play, he decides that since he "cannot prove himself a lover", he will be "determined to prove a villain".

At the close of the previous scene, he has decided that one way to advance his cause to become king is to marry into the powerful family of the Earl of Warwick:

I'll marry Warwick's youngest daughter—

What though I killed her husband, and her father?

The scene that follows dramatizes this extraordinary decision by having Lady Anne enter with the body of her father-in-law, King Henry VI, whom Richard had murdered. The wooing takes place with this gruesome prop on stage for the whole scene.

ACT 1, SCENE 2

Enter [Gentlemen and Bearers with] the corpse
of Henry the Sixth, with Halberds[2] to guard
it, Lady Anne being the mourner.

ANNE   Set down, set down your honourable load—
If honour may be shrouded in a hearse—
Whilst I awhile obsequiously lament
Th'untimely fall of virtuous Lancaster.[3]
Poor key-cold figure of a holy king,
Pale ashes of the House of Lancaster,
Thou bloodless remnant of that royal blood.
Be it lawful that I invocate thy ghost
To hear the lamentations of poor Anne,
Wife to thy Edward, to thy slaughtered son,
Stabbed by the selfsame hand that made these
    wounds.
Lo, in these windows[4] that let forth thy life
I pour the helpless balm of my poor eyes.

O, cursèd be the hand that made these holes;
Cursèd the heart that had the heart to do it;
Cursèd the blood that let this blood from hence.
More direful hap[5] betide that hated wretch
That makes us wretched by the death of thee
Than I can wish to adders, spiders, toads,
Or any creeping venomed thing that lives.
If ever he have child, abortive be it—
Prodigious,[6] and untimely brought to light,
Whose ugly and unnatural aspect
May fright the hopeful mother at the view,
And that be heir to his unhappiness.
If ever he have wife, let her be made
More miserable by the death of him
Than I am made by my young lord and thee.
Come now towards Chertsey[7] with your holy load,
Taken from Paul's to be interrèd there;
And still, as you are weary of the weight,
Rest you, while I lament King Henry's corpse.
                [The Bearers take up the coffin.] Enter Richard.

RICHARD   Stay, you that bear the corpse, and set it down.
ANNE   What black magician conjures up this fiend
                To stop devoted charitable deeds?
RICHARD   Villains! set down the corpse, or by Saint Paul
                I'll make a corpse of him that disobeys!
HALBERDIER   *[lowers his halbert to stop Richard]*
                My lord, stand back and let the coffin pass.
RICHARD   Unmannered dog, stand thou when I command!
                Advance thy halberd higher than my breast,
                Or, by Saint Paul, I'll strike thee to my foot,
                And spurn[8] upon thee, beggar, for thy boldness.
                    [The Bearers set down the coffin.]

ANNE	What, do you tremble? Are you all afraid?
	Alas, I blame you not, for you are mortal,
	And mortal eyes cannot endure the devil.
	Avaunt,[9] thou dreadful minister of hell!
	Thou hadst but[10] power over his mortal body,
	His soul thou canst not have—therefore begone.
RICHARD	Sweet saint, for charity be not so curst.
ANNE	Foul devil, for God's sake hence, and trouble us not;
	For thou hast made the happy earth thy hell,
	Filled it with cursing cries and deep exclaims.
	If thou delight to view thy heinous deeds,
	Behold this pattern of thy butcheries.
	O gentlemen, see; see dead Henry's wounds
	Open their congealed mouths and bleed afresh.[11]
	Blush, blush, thou lump of foul deformity,
	For 'tis thy presence that exhales[12] this blood
	From cold and empty veins where no blood dwells;
	Thy deeds inhuman and unnatural
	Provokes this deluge most unnatural.
	O God, which this blood mad'st, revenge his death!
	O earth, which this blood drink'st, revenge his death!
	Either heaven with lightning strike the murderer dead,
	Or earth gape open wide and eat him quick,[13]
	As thou dost swallow up this good King's blood
	Which his hell-governed arm hath butchered.
RICHARD	Lady, you know no rules of charity,
	Which renders good for bad, blessings for curses.
ANNE	Villain, thou know'st nor law of God nor man.
	No beast so fierce but knows[14] some touch of pity.
RICHARD	But I know none, and therefore am no beast.
ANNE	O wonderful, when devils tell the truth!
RICHARD	More wonderful, when angels are so angry.

	Vouchsafe,[15] divine perfection of a woman,
	Of these supposed crimes, to give me leave,
	By circumstance,[16] but to acquit myself.
ANNE	Vouchsafe, defused[17] infection of a man,
	Of these known evils, but to give me leave,
	By circumstance, to accuse thy cursed self.
RICHARD	Fairer than tongue can name thee, let me have
	Some patient leisure to excuse myself.
ANNE	Fouler than heart can think thee, thou canst make
	No excuse current but to hang thyself.
RICHARD	By such despair I should accuse myself.

. . . .

ANNE	Didst thou not kill this King?
RICHARD	I grant ye.
ANNE	Dost grant me, hedgehog?[18] Then God grant me too
	Thou mayst be damnèd for that wicked deed.
	Oh, he was gentle, mild, and virtuous.
RICHARD	The better for the King of Heaven that hath him.
ANNE	He is in heaven, where thou shalt never come.
RICHARD	Let him thank me that holp to send him thither,
	For he was fitter for that place than earth.
ANNE	And thou unfit for any place but hell.
RICHARD	Yes, one place else, if you will hear me name it.
ANNE	Some dungeon!
RICHARD	Your bed-chamber.
ANNE	Ill rest betide the chamber where thou liest.
RICHARD	So will it, madam, till I lie with you.
ANNE	I hope so.
RICHARD	I know so. But, gentle Lady Anne,
	To leave this keen encounter of our wits,
	And fall something into a slower method—
	Is not the causer of the timeless deaths

	Of these Plantagenets,[19] Henry and Edward,
	As blameful as the executioner?
ANNE	Thou wast the cause and most accursed effect.
RICHARD	Your beauty was the cause of that effect:
	Your beauty, that did haunt me in my sleep
	To undertake the death of all the world,
	So I might live one hour in your sweet bosom.
ANNE	If I thought that, I tell thee, homicide,
	These nails should rend that beauty from my cheeks.
RICHARD	These eyes could not endure that beauty's wrack;
	You should not blemish it if I stood by.
	As all the world is cheered by the sun,
	So I by that; it is my day, my life.
ANNE	Black night o'ershade thy day, and death thy life.
RICHARD	Curse not thyself, fair creature; thou art both.
ANNE	I would I were, to be revenged on thee.
RICHARD	It is a quarrel most unnatural,
	To be revenged on him that loveth thee.
ANNE	It is a quarrel just and reasonable,
	To be revenged on him that killed my husband.
RICHARD	He that bereft thee, lady, of thy husband,
	Did it to help thee to a better husband.
ANNE	His better doth not breathe upon the earth.
RICHARD	He lives that loves thee better than he could.
ANNE	Name him.
RICHARD	Plantagenet.
ANNE	Why, that was he.
RICHARD	The self-same name, but one of better nature.
ANNE	Where is he?
RICHARD	Here. [She] *spits at him.*
	Why dost thou spit at me?
ANNE	Would it were mortal poison, for thy sake.

RICHARD	Never came poison from so sweet a place.
ANNE	Never hung poison on a fouler toad.
	Out of my sight! Thou dost infect mine eyes.
RICHARD	Thine eyes, sweet lady, have infected mine.
ANNE	Would they were basilisks,[20] to strike thee dead.
RICHARD	I would they were, that I might die at once;
	For now they kill me with a living death.

. . . .

I never sued to friend nor enemy;

My tongue could never learn sweet smoothing word;

But now thy beauty is proposed my fee,

My proud heart sues, and prompts my tongue to
  speak.

She looks scornfully at him.

Teach not thy lip such scorn; for it was made

For kissing, lady, not for such contempt.

If thy revengeful heart cannot forgive,

Lo, here I lend thee this sharp-pointed sword—

Which, if thou please to hide in this true breast,

And let the soul forth that adoreth thee—

I lay it naked to the deadly stroke,

And humbly beg the death upon my knee.

[He kneels, and] lays his breast open; she offers at
  [it] with his sword.

Nay, do not pause, for I did kill King Henry—

But 'twas thy beauty that provokèd me.

Nay, now dispatch: 'twas I that stabbed young
  Edward—

But 'twas thy heavenly face that set me on.

She falls the sword.

Take up the sword again, or take up me.

ANNE	Arise, dissembler; though I wish thy death, *[He rises.]*

	I will not be thy executioner.
RICHARD	Then bid me kill myself, and I will do it.
ANNE	I have already.
RICHARD	That was in thy rage.
	Speak it again, and even with the word,
	This hand, which for thy love did kill thy love,
	Shall for thy love kill a far truer love:
	To both their deaths shalt thou be accessory.
ANNE	I would I knew thy heart.
RICHARD	'Tis figured in my tongue.
ANNE	I fear me both are false.
RICHARD	Then never was man true.
ANNE	Well, well, put up your sword.
RICHARD	Say then my peace is made.
ANNE	That shalt thou know hereafter.
RICHARD	But shall I live in hope?
ANNE	All men, I hope, live so.
RICHARD	Vouchsafe[21] to wear this ring.
ANNE	To take is not to give.[22] [*He puts on the ring.*]
RICHARD	Look how my ring encompasseth thy finger:
	Even so thy breast encloseth my poor heart;
	Wear both of them, for both of them are thine.
	And if thy poor devoted servant[23] may
	But beg one favour at thy gracious hand,
	Thou dost confirm his happiness for ever.
ANNE	What is it?
RICHARD	That it may please you leave these sad designs
	To him that hath most cause to be a mourner,
	And presently repair to Crosby House,
	Where, after I have solemnly interred
	At Chertsey Monastery this noble King,
	And wet his grave with my repentant tears,

	I will with all expedient duty see you.
	For divers unknown reasons, I beseech you
	Grant me this boon.
ANNE	With all my heart; and much it joys me too,
	To see you are become so penitent.
	Tressel and Berkeley, go along with me.
RICHARD	Bid me farewell.
ANNE	'Tis more than you deserve;
	But since you teach me how to flatter you,
	Imagine I have said farewell already.
	Exeunt [Gentlemen] with Anne.
RICHARD	Sirs, take up the corpse.
GENTLEMAN	Towards Chertsey, noble lord?
RICHARD	No, to Whitefriars; there attend my coming.
	Exeunt [Halberds with] corpse.
	Was ever woman in this humour wooed?
	Was ever woman in this humour won?
	I'll have her—but I will not keep her long.

....

My dukedom to a beggarly denier,[24]
I do mistake my person all this while!
Upon my life, she finds—although I cannot—
Myself to be a marvellous proper man.
I'll be at charges for a looking-glass,
And entertain a score or two of tailors
To study fashions to adorn my body.
Since I am crept in favour with myself,
I will maintain it with some little cost.
But first I'll turn yon fellow in his grave,
And then return lamenting to my love.
Shine out, fair sun, till I have bought a glass,
That I may see my shadow as I pass.   *Exit.*

Troilus and Cressida

If Richard is Shakespeare's quintessential anti-hero, *Troilus and Cressida* is his anti-heroic play. The Trojan War is usually seen as an epic battle between heroes; Shakespeare's play, however, is far from heroic. Chaucer's great poem *Troilus and Criseyde* celebrates a late legend from the war, the love of the Trojan Troilus for Cressida, whose father, Calchas, had sworn allegiance to the Greeks; there is thus an echo of the feuding families of *Romeo and Juliet* in the background. In what is perhaps his darkest play, the war is reduced to a plot where "all the argument is a whore and a cuckold". In such an atmosphere, the love of Troilus and Cressida is doomed; each, in their own way, contributes to the failure through lack of faith – in themselves and in each other.

In this early soliloquy, Cressida responds to the persuasions of her sentimental, but corrupt, uncle, Pandarus (from whom the term "pander" is derived); she loves Troilus more than she publicly admits, but is afraid that if she yields to him he will immediately lose interest in her.

ACT 1, SCENE 2

CRESSIDA Words, vows, gifts, tears, and love's full sacrifice
He offers in another's enterprise;
But more in Troilus thousandfold I see
Than in the glass[1] of Pandar's praise may be.
Yet hold I off. Women are angels, wooing;
Things won are done; joy's soul lies in the doing.
That she beloved knows naught that knows not this:
Men prize the thing ungained more than it is.
That she was never yet that ever knew

Love got so sweet as when desire did sue.[2]
Therefore this maxim out of love I teach:
"Achievement is command; ungained, beseech."[3]
Then, though my heart's content firm love doth
   bear,
Nothing of that shall from mine eyes appear.   *Exit.*

The lovers are about to meet for a night together. For all his passionate claims of love, Troilus fears that his expectations will be disappointed, both in his own performance and in Cressida's fidelity. Pandarus delights, almost voyeuristically, in bringing them together. Unlike the lyrical outpourings of Shakespeare's earlier lovers, Romeo and Juliet, these two are determinedly prosaic.

ACT 3, SCENE 2

TROILUS   I am giddy; expectation whirls me round.
            Th'imaginary relish is so sweet
            That it enchants my sense. What will it be,
            When that the wat'ry palates[4] taste indeed
            Love's thrice-repurèd nectar? Death, I fear me,
            Swooning destruction, or some joy too fine,
            Too subtle-potent, tuned too sharp in sweetness,
            For the capacity of my ruder powers.
            I fear it much; and I do fear besides
            That I shall lose distinction in my joys,
            As doth a battle, when they charge on heaps
            The enemy flying.
                Enter Pandarus.

PANDARUS   She's making her ready; she'll come straight. You
            must be witty now. She does so blush, and fetches
            her wind so short, as if she were frayed with a

sprite.[5] I'll fetch her. It is the prettiest villain;[6] she fetches her breath as short as a new-ta'en sparrow.

Exit Pandarus.

TROILUS   Even such a passion doth embrace my bosom.
My heart beats thicker than a feverous pulse,
And all my powers do their bestowing lose,
Like vassalage[7] at unawares encount'ring
The eye of majesty.

Enter Pandarus, and Cressida [veiled].

PANDARUS   [*to Cressida*] Come, come, what need you blush? Shame's a baby. [*to Troilus*] Here she is now. Swear the oaths now to her that you have sworn to me. [*Cressida draws back.*] What, are you gone again? You must be watched[8] ere you be made tame, must you? Come your ways, come your ways; an you draw backward, we'll put you i'the fills.[9] [*to Troilus*] Why do you not speak to her? Come, draw this curtain and let's see your picture. [*He unveils Cressida.*] Alas the day, how loath you are to offend daylight! An 'twere dark, you'd close sooner. [*to Troilus*] So, so; rub on,[10] and kiss the mistress. [*They kiss.*] How now, a kiss in fee-farm![11] Build there, carpenter, the air is sweet. Nay, you shall fight your hearts out ere I part you. The falcon as the tercel,[12] for all the ducks i'the river. Go to, go to.

TROILUS   You have bereft me of all words, lady.

PANDARUS   Words pay no debts, give her deeds; but she'll bereave you o'the deeds too, if she call your activity in question. [*They kiss.*] What, billing[13] again? Here's "In witness whereof the parties interchangeably".[14] Come in, come in; I'll go get a fire.

[Exit.]

CRESSIDA	Will you walk in, my lord?
TROILUS	O Cressid, how often have I wished me thus!
CRESSIDA	Wished, my lord? The gods grant—O my lord!
TROILUS	What should they grant? What makes this pretty abruption?[15] What too-curious dreg[16] espies my sweet lady in the fountain of our love?
CRESSIDA	More dregs than water, if my fears have eyes.
TROILUS	Fears make devils of cherubims;[17] they never see truly.
CRESSIDA	Blind fear, that seeing reason leads, finds safer footing than blind reason, stumbling without fear. To fear the worst oft cures the worse.
TROILUS	O, let my lady apprehend no fear. In all Cupid's pageant there is presented no monster.
CRESSIDA	Nor nothing monstrous neither?
TROILUS	Nothing but our undertakings, when we vow to weep seas, live in fire, eat rocks, tame tigers, thinking it harder for our mistress to devise imposition[18] enough than for us to undergo any difficulty imposed. This is the monstrosity in love, lady, that the will is infinite and the execution confined; that the desire is boundless and the act a slave to limit.
CRESSIDA	They say all lovers swear more performance than they are able, and yet reserve an ability that they never perform, vowing more than the perfection of ten and discharging less than the tenth part of one. They that have the voice of lions and the act of hares, are they not monsters?
TROILUS	Are there such? Such are not we. Praise us as we are tasted, allow us as we prove.

Measure for Measure

Measure for Measure and *Troilus and Cressida* are known as "problem" plays, since, although the plots do not culminate in the deaths of their protagonists, they are far from being comic. Both explore the darker, more obsessive side of love, and in both, the men see women as inevitably fickle. In this short abstract, the Lord Angelo, put in charge of Vienna by the absent Duke, responds to a visit by Isabella. Angelo has sentenced Isabella's brother to death for fornication – he has made his fiancée pregnant – and discovers to his dismay that he has fallen for Isabella's attractions in the same way. His response is the more shocking because Isabella is a novitiate, about to become a nun. Shakespeare explores the psychology of the abuse of power, and the perverse sexual attraction that culminates in rape: at their next meeting he offers to trade her brother's life for sex with her.

ACT 2, SCENE 2

ISABELLA   Save your honour.

　　　　　　　　　　　　　　　　　　[Exeunt all but Angelo.]

ANGELO   From thee; even from thy virtue!
　　　　　　　What's this? What's this? Is this her fault or mine?
　　　　　　　The tempter or the tempted, who sins most? Ha?
　　　　　　　Not she; nor doth she tempt; but it is I
　　　　　　　That, lying by the violet in the sun,
　　　　　　　Do as the carrion does, not as the flower,
　　　　　　　Corrupt with virtuous season.[1] Can it be
　　　　　　　That modesty may more betray our sense[2]
　　　　　　　Than woman's lightness?[3] Having waste ground
　　　　　　　　　enough,

Shall we desire to raze the sanctuary
And pitch our evils there? O fie, fie, fie!
What dost thou, or what art thou, Angelo?
Dost thou desire her foully for those things
That make her good? O, let her brother live!
Thieves for their robbery have authority
When judges steal themselves. What, do I love her,
That I desire to hear her speak again
And feast upon her eyes? What is't I dream on?
O cunning enemy, that, to catch a saint,[4]
With saints dost bait thy hook! Most dangerous
Is that temptation that doth goad us on
To sin in loving virtue. Never could the strumpet,
With all her double vigour, art, and nature,
Once stir my temper; but this virtuous maid
Subdues me quite. Ever till now,
When men were fond, I smiled and wondered how.

Othello

Written at about the same time as the problem plays, *Othello* takes the difficulty of the course of true love to a tragic conclusion. As in the problem plays, Shakespeare shows how the male eye has a disconcerting tendency to see women in absolutes, as either divine or hellish, as angels or as whores. Othello is a study in a man brilliant in one field – the art of war – but stumbling in another – the art of love. He is very much the outsider in Venice, as both a black man and a product of a profoundly different culture; those around him habitually describe him as "the Moor". The Viennese want only one thing from him – his capacity to wage war, not love. While Desdemona delights in his difference, Othello is haunted by Iago, Shakespeare's ultimate villain, outdoing even Richard III in his callous delight in appearing to all to be honest, while manipulating and inflicting pain on others.

Othello is roused from bed in the inn where he is spending the first night of his elopement, and he is brought urgently to the Duke of Venice. The Turks are threatening the island of Cyprus, with the result that the Venetians have desperate need for the skills of Othello as a general; at the same time, Brabantio, Desdemona's father, is urging the Senate to take action against Othello for "bewitching" his daughter. Othello describes his courtship of Desdemona in terms that rather charmingly make clear the fact that she effectively wooed him.

ACT 1, SCENE 3

OTHELLO   So justly to your grave ears I'll present
            How I did thrive in this fair lady's love,
            And she in mine.

DUKE	Say it, Othello.
OTHELLO	Her father loved me, oft invited me,

Still[1] questioned me the story of my life
From year to year—the battles, sieges, fortunes,
That I have passed.
I ran it through, even from my boyish days
To th'very moment that he bade me tell it;
Wherein I spake of most disastrous chances,
Of moving[2] accidents by flood and field,
Of hair-breadth 'scapes i'th' imminent deadly
     breach,[3]
Of being taken by the insolent foe
And sold to slavery, of my redemption thence . . .
These things to hear
Would Desdemona seriously incline;
But still the house affairs would draw her thence,
Which ever as she could with haste dispatch
She'd come again, and with a greedy ear
Devour up my discourse. Which I observing,
Took once a pliant hour[4] and found good means
To draw from her a prayer of earnest heart
That I would all my pilgrimage dilate,[5]
Whereof by parcels she had something heard,
But not intentively.[6] I did consent,
And often did beguile her of her tears
When I did speak of some distressful stroke
That my youth suffered. My story being done,
She gave me for my pains a world of sighs;
She swore, in faith, 'twas strange, 'twas passing
     strange;
'Twas pitiful, 'twas wondrous pitiful.
She wished she had not heard it, yet she wished

That heaven had made her such a man. She
    thanked me,
And bade me, if I had a friend that loved her,
I should but teach him how to tell my story,
And that would woo her. Upon this hint I spake:
She loved me for the dangers I had passed,
And I loved her that she did pity them.
This only is the witchcraft[7] I have used.
Here comes the lady; let her witness it.
    Enter Desdemona, Iago, [and] Attendants.

DUKE   I think this tale would win my daughter too.
Good Brabantio,
Take up this mangled matter at the best.[8]
Men do their broken weapons rather use
Than their bare hands.

BRABANTIO   I pray you, hear her speak.
If she confess that she was half the wooer,
Destruction on my head, if my bad blame
Light on the man! Come hither, gentle mistress.
Do you perceive in all this noble company
Where most you owe obedience?

DESDEMONA   My noble father,
I do perceive here a divided duty.
To you I am bound for life and education;
My life and education both do learn[9] me
How to respect you. You are the lord of duty;[10]
I am hitherto your daughter. But here's my
    husband,
And so much duty as my mother show'd
To you, preferring you before her father,
So much I challenge that I may profess
Due to the Moor my lord.

BRABANTIO   God be with you! I have done.

Please it your Grace, on to the state affairs.

I had rather to adopt a child than get it.

Come hither, Moor.

> [*Perhaps he joins the hands of Desdemona*
> *and Othello.*]

I here do give thee that with all my heart

Which, but thou hast already, with all my heart

I would keep from thee.

They discuss where Desdemona should reside while Othello is at war; the Duke suggests that she stay with her father, to which Brabantio responds.

BRABANTIO   I will not have it so.

OTHELLO   Nor I.

DESDEMONA   Nor I. I would not there reside,

To put my father in impatient thoughts

By being in his eye. Most gracious Duke,

To my unfolding lend your prosperous ear,

And let me find a charter[11] in your voice

To assist my simpleness.

DUKE   What would you, Desdemona?

DESDEMONA   That I did love the Moor to live with him,

My downright violence and storm of fortunes[12]

May trumpet to the world. My heart's subdued

Even to the very quality of my lord.

I saw Othello's visage in his mind,[13]

And to his honours and his valiant parts[14]

Did I my soul and fortunes consecrate.

So that, dear lords, if I be left behind

A moth[15] of peace, and he go to the war,

	The rites[16] for why I love him are bereft me,
	And I a heavy interim shall support
	By his dear absence. Let me go with him.
OTHELLO	Let her have your voice.
	Vouch with me, heaven, I therefore beg it not
	To please the palate of my appetite,
	Nor to comply with heat[17]—the young affects
	In me defunct—and proper satisfaction,
	But to be free and bounteous to her mind.
	And heaven defend your good souls that you think
	I will your serious and great business scant[18]
	When she is with me. No, when light-winged toys
	Of feathered Cupid seel[19] with wanton dullness
	My speculative and officed instruments,[20]
	That my disports[21] corrupt and taint my business,
	Let housewives make a skillet of my helm,
	And all indign[22] and base adversities
	Make head against my estimation![23]
DUKE	Be it as you shall privately determine,
	Either for her stay or going. Th'affair cries haste,
	And speed must answer't: you must hence tonight.

At the end of this scene, Iago is left on stage with the foolish Rodrigo, a young nobleman who dotes on Desdemona. Iago, using him for his own purposes, promises to pass on rich gifts to her; he urges Rodrigo to sell his lands. In the process, Iago reveals his debased view of love.

RODRIGO	What should I do? I confess it is my shame to be so
	fond, but it is not in my virtue to amend it.
IAGO	Virtue? a fig![24] 'Tis in ourselves that we are thus or
	thus. Our bodies are our gardens, to the which our

wills are gardeners; so that if we will plant nettles or sow lettuce, set hyssop[25] and weed up thyme, supply it with one gender of herbs or distract it with many, either to have it sterile with idleness or manured with industry—why, the power and corrigible authority[26] of this lies in our wills. If the balance of our lives had not one scale of reason to poise[27] another of sensuality, the blood and baseness of our natures would conduct us to most preposterous conclusions. But we have reason to cool our raging motions, our carnal stings, our unbitted[28] lusts; whereof I take this, that you call "love", to be a sect or scion.[29]

RODRIGO It cannot be.

IAGO It is merely a lust of the blood and a permission of the will. . . . It cannot be long that Desdemona should continue her love to the Moor—put money in thy purse—nor he his to her. It was a violent commencement, and thou shalt see an answerable sequestration[30]—put but money in thy purse. These Moors are changeable in their wills—fill thy purse with money. The food that to him now is as luscious as locusts,[31] shall be to him shortly as bitter as coloquintida.[32] She must change for youth; when she is sated with his body, she will find the error of her choice. She must have change, she must. Therefore put money in thy purse. . . . If sanctimony[33] and a frail vow betwixt an erring barbarian and a supersubtle Venetian be not too hard for my wits and all the tribe of hell, thou shalt enjoy her.

Desdemona, with winds favouring her ship, reaches the island of Cyprus before Othello. She greets him as he arrives.

ACT 2, SCENE 1

OTHELLO   O my fair warrior!

DESDEMONA   My dear Othello!

OTHELLO   It gives me wonder great as my content

To see you here before me. O my soul's joy,

If after every tempest come such calms,

May the winds blow till they have wakened death,

And let the labouring bark³⁴ climb hills of seas

Olympus-high,³⁵ and duck again as low

As hell's from heaven! If it were now to die,

'Twere now to be most happy, for I fear

My soul hath her content so absolute

That not another comfort like to this

Succeeds in unknown fate.

DESDEMONA   The heavens forbid

But that our loves and comforts should increase,

Even as our days do grow!

OTHELLO   Amen to that, sweet powers!

I cannot speak enough of this content.

It stops me here; [*touching his breast*] it is too much

of joy.

And this, and this, [*They kiss.*] the greatest discords

be

That e'er our hearts shall make!

IAGO   [*aside*]   O, you are well tuned now!

But I'll set down the pegs that make this music,

As honest as I am.

Iago begins his manipulation of Othello by a brilliant series of hints and feints, stimulating Othello's curiosity by innuendo, never saying anything directly, and seeming to resist telling the "truth". He indirectly suggests that Othello's lieutenant, Cassio, is having an affair with Desdemona. When he finally makes a direct statement about jealousy, Iago plays upon Othello's sense of being an outsider, one who is unfamiliar with the ways of Venice, and its culture, so different from his own.

ACT 3, SCENE 3

IAGO   Good name in man and woman, dear my lord,
Is the immediate jewel of their souls.
Who steals my purse steals trash; 'tis something,
    nothing;
'Twas mine, 'tis his, and has been slave to thousands;
But he that filches from me my good name
Robs me of that which not enriches him
And makes me poor indeed.

OTHELLO   By heaven, I'll know thy thoughts.

IAGO   You cannot, if my heart were in your hand,
Nor shall not, whilst 'tis in my custody.

OTHELLO   Ha?

IAGO   Oh, beware, my lord, of jealousy.
It is the green-eyed monster, which doth mock
The meat it feeds on. That cuckold[36] lives in bliss
Who, certain of his fate, loves not his wronger;
But Oh, what damnèd minutes tells he o'er
Who dotes, yet doubts, suspects, yet fondly loves!

OTHELLO   O misery!

IAGO   Poor and content is rich, and rich enough,
But riches fineless[37] is as poor as winter
To him that ever fears he shall be poor.
Good God, the souls of all my tribe defend
From jealousy!

OTHELLO   Why, why is this?
Think'st thou I'd make a life of jealousy,

To follow still the changes of the moon
With fresh suspicions? No! To be once in doubt
Is once to be resolved.[38] Exchange me for a goat
When I shall turn the business of my soul
To such exsufflicate and blown[39] surmises
Matching thy inference. 'Tis not to make me jealous
To say my wife is fair, feeds well, loves company,
Is free of speech, sings, plays, and dances well;
Where virtue is, these are more virtuous.
Nor from mine own weak merits will I draw
The smallest fear or doubt of her revolt,
For she had eyes and chose me. No, Iago,
I'll see before I doubt; when I doubt, prove;
And on the proof, there is no more but this—
Away at once with love or jealousy!

IAGO   I am glad of this, for now I shall have reason
To show the love and duty that I bear you
With franker spirit. Therefore, as I am bound,
Receive it from me. I speak not yet of proof.
Look to your wife; observe her well with Cassio;
Wear your eye thus, not jealous nor secure.
I would not have your free and noble nature
Out of self-bounty be abused. Look to't.
I know our country disposition[40] well;
In Venice they do let God see the pranks
They dare not show their husbands; their best
    conscience
Is not to leave't undone, but keep't unknown.

OTHELLO   Dost thou say so?

IAGO   She did deceive her father, marrying you;
And when she seem'd to shake and fear your looks,
She loved them most.

OTHELLO	And so she did.
IAGO	Why, go to then!

She that, so young, could give out such a seeming,
To seel her father's eyes up close as oak—
He thought 'twas witchcraft! But I am much to
    blame;
I humbly do beseech you of your pardon
For too much loving you.

OTHELLO   I am bound to thee forever.

Iago continues his assault on Othello, increasingly convincing him of Desemona's infidelity. After Othello leaves, Emilia, Iago's wife and Desdemona's maid, tells Iago that she has picked up an intricately woven handkerchief that Desdemona dropped – it was a gift from Othello to Desdemona, and is seen as a symbol of their love. Iago seizes it in delight.

IAGO   Be not acknown[41] on't; I have use for it.
Go, leave me.   *Exit Emilia.*
I will in Cassio's lodging lose this napkin
And let him find it. Trifles light as air
Are to the jealous confirmations strong
As proofs of Holy Writ. This may do something.
The Moor already changes with my poison.
Dangerous conceits[42] are in their natures poisons,
Which at the first are scarce found to distaste,
But with a little act upon the blood[43]
Burn like the mines of sulphur. I did say so.
    Enter Othello.
Look, where he comes! Not poppy, nor
    mandragora,[44]
Nor all the drowsy syrups of the world

Shall ever medicine thee to that sweet sleep
Which thou owed'st yesterday.

Othello's actions have become more erratic and violent as his
suspicions increase and seem to be confirmed, thanks to Iago's
machinations. Othello strikes Desdemona in public. She remains
obedient, and asks Emilia to put her wedding sheets on the bed
in preparation for her husband's coming. Emilia prepares her for
bed, as the two women share an intimate discussion; Emilia's earthy
pragmatism sharply contrasts with Desdemona's idealism. Once
again, Shakespeare associates melancholy in love with music.

ACT 4, SCENE 3

DESDEMONA   [*sings*] "The poor soul sat sighing by a sycamore tree,
                            Sing all a green willow;[45]
                    Her hand on her bosom, her head on her knee,
                        Sing willow, willow, willow.
                    The fresh streams ran by her, and murmured her
                        moans,
                    Sing willow, willow, willow;
                    Her salt tears fell from her, and softened the
                        stones—"
            Lay by these.
                [*sings*] "Sing willow, willow, willow—"
            Prithee, hie thee; he'll come anon.
                [*sings*] "Sing all a green willow must be my
                    garland.
                Let nobody blame him; his scorn I approve—"
            Nay, that's not next. Hark, who is't that knocks?
EMILIA   It's the wind.
DESDEMONA   [*sings*] "I called my love false love; but what said he
                            then?

Sing willow, willow, willow;
    If I court more women, you'll couch with more
    men."
So get thee gone; good night. Mine eyes do itch;
Doth that bode weeping?

EMILIA   'Tis neither here nor there.

DESDEMONA I have heard it said so. O, these men, these men!
Dost thou in conscience think—tell me, Emilia—
That there be women do abuse their husbands
In such gross kind?

EMILIA   There be some such, no question.

DESDEMONA Wouldst thou do such a deed for all the world?

EMILIA Why, would not you?

DESDEMONA   No, by this heavenly light!

EMILIA Nor I neither by this heavenly light; I might do't as
well i'th' dark.

DESDEMONA Wouldst thou do such a deed for all the world?

EMILIA The world's a huge thing. It is a great price for a
small vice.

DESDEMONA By my troth, I think thou wouldst not.

EMILIA In troth, I think I should, and undo't when I had done.
Marry, I would not do such a thing for a joint-ring,[46]
nor for measures of lawn,[47] nor for gowns, petticoats,
nor caps, nor any petty exhibition.[48] But for all the
whole world? Ud's pity,[49] who would not make her
husband a cuckold to make him a monarch? I should
venture purgatory for't.

DESDEMONA Beshrew me if I would do such a wrong
For the whole world.

EMILIA Why, the wrong is but a wrong i'th' world; and having
the world for your labour, 'tis a wrong in your own
world, and you might quickly make it right.

DESDEMONA	I do not think there is any such woman.
EMILIA	Yes, a dozen, and as many

EMILIA
To th'vantage as would store the world they played
for.[50]
But I do think it is their husbands' faults
If wives do fall. Say that they slack their duties
And pour our treasures into foreign laps;[51]
Or else break out in peevish jealousies,
Throwing restraint upon us; or say they strike us,
Or scant our former having in despite?[52]
Why, we have galls,[53] and though we have some
grace,
Yet have we some revenge. Let husbands know
Their wives have sense[54] like them; they see and
smell,
And have their palates both for sweet and sour,
As husbands have. What is it that they do
When they change us for others? Is it sport?[55]
I think it is. And doth affection[56] breed it?
I think it doth. Is't frailty that thus errs?
It is so too. And have not we affections,
Desires for sport, and frailty, as men have?
Then let them use us well; else let them know,
The ills we do, their ills instruct us so.

DESDEMONA
Good night, good night. God me such uses send,
Not to pick bad from bad, but by bad mend!

Exeunt.

Othello enters the bedroom, determined to kill his wife. His language, calmer than it was, still shows the way in which he is torn between his determination and the love he feels as he sees her asleep.

ACT 5, SCENE 2

Enter Othello [with a candle, to Desdemona in her bed]

OTHELLO   It is the cause, it is the cause, my soul.

Let me not name it to you, you chaste stars!

It is the cause. Yet I'll not shed her blood,

Nor scar that whiter skin of hers than snow,

And smooth as monumental alabaster.[57]

Yet she must die, else she'll betray more men.

Put out the light,[58] and then put out the light.

If I quench thee, thou flaming minister,

I can again thy former light restore,

Should I repent me; but once put out thy light,

Thou cunningest pattern of excelling nature,

I know not where is that Promethean[59] heat

That can thy light relume. When I have plucked
    thy rose,

I cannot give it vital growth again;

It must needs wither. I'll smell it on the tree.
    [He kisses her.]

Oh, balmy breath, that dost almost persuade

Justice to break her sword! One more, one more.

Be thus when thou art dead, and I will kill thee,

And love thee after. One more, and that's the last.
    [Kisses her.]

So sweet was ne'er so fatal. I must weep,

But they are cruel tears. This sorrow's heavenly;

It strikes where it doth love.

Othello strangles Desdemona; he is discovered, and after Emilia reveals the truth, that Iago has deceived him, Othello pulls out a concealed dagger and speaks his last words. While he acknowledges his error in believing Desdemona to be unfaithful, we may feel that he has still not understood fully how easy it was for Iago to play upon his vulnerability as an outsider.

OTHELLO Soft you. A word or two before you go.
I have done the state some service, and they know't.
No more of that. I pray you, in your letters,
When you shall these unlucky deeds relate,
Speak of me as I am; nothing extenuate,
Nor set down aught in malice. Then must you speak
Of one that loved not wisely but too well;
Of one not easily jealous, but, being wrought,[60]
Perplexed in the extreme; of one whose hand,
Like the base Indian,[61] threw a pearl away
Richer than all his tribe; of one whose subdued eyes,
Albeit unused to the melting mood,
Drops tears as fast as the Arabian trees
Their medicinal gum.[62] Set you down this;
And say besides, that in Aleppo once,
Where a malignant and a turban'd Turk
Beat a Venetian and traduced the state,
I took by the throat the circumcised dog
And smote him, thus.
                    [*He stabs himself.*]
LODOVICO Oh, bloody period!
GRATIANO   All that is spoke is marred.
OTHELLO I kissed thee ere I killed thee. No way but this,
Killing myself, to die upon a kiss.   *Dies.*

Antony and Cleopatra

Shakespeare's last plays offer some relief from the dark world of the problem plays and tragedies. *Antony and Cleopatra* is a tragedy on a grand scale, but its ending is far less dark than that of *Othello*, where the protagonist's final words may be taken to suggest that he has never fully understood the degree to which he was vulnerable to the machinations of Iago. *The Winter's Tale* records a jealousy even more obsessive and potentially destructive than Othello's, but the play also offers antidotes in its younger lovers, and in an ending that is at once fantastic and deeply positive.

In *Antony and Cleopatra*, Shakespeare seems to have been fascinated by a central question. What kind of love did the two protagonists feel, sufficient to give up power over half the world: sufficient to make Antony desert his men in a battle at sea and follow Cleopatra's barge? What kind of woman was Cleopatra to inspire such an action? Not surprisingly there are no simple answers: both lovers are splendid and both are flawed. The initial view of Antony is that of the Roman soldiers, who see things very much in black and white: Antony dotes on Cleopatra, and she has bewitched him. But when the lovers enter, Cleopatra asking how much he loves her, his answer is splendid: real love cannot be quantified.

ACT 1, SCENE 1

PHILO   Nay, but this dotage of our general's
           O'erflows the measure. Those his goodly eyes,
           That o'er the files and musters of the war
           Have glowed like plated Mars,[1] now bend, now turn
           The office and devotion of their view
           Upon a tawny front.[2] His captain's heart,

Which in the scuffles of great fights hath burst
The buckles on his breast, reneges all temper[3]
And is become the bellows and the fan
To cool a gipsy's lust.

> *Flourish. Enter Antony, Cleopatra, her Ladies*
> *[Charmian and Iras], the train, with Eunuchs*
> *fanning her.*

Look where they come!
Take but good note, and you shall see in him
The triple pillar[4] of the world transformed
Into a strumpet's fool. Behold and see.

CLEOPATRA   If it be love indeed, tell me how much.

ANTONY   There's beggary in the love that can be reckoned.

CLEOPATRA   I'll set a bourn[5] how far to be beloved.

ANTONY   Then must thou needs find out new heaven, new
earth.

Cleopatra can be seen as anything from selfishly manipulative (the traditional Roman view) to insecure, working hard to keep Antony's interest as she ages. At one stage she describes her changeableness as "sweating labour". In this brief scene we see her working hard at her arts of love, deliberately choosing to challenge Antony by being contrary; no wonder the Roman Philo described her as paradoxically heating and cooling Antony at the same time: as both "bellows" and "fan".

ACT 1, SCENE 3

> *Enter Cleopatra, Charmian, Alexas and Iras.*

CLEOPATRA   Where is he?

CHARMIAN   I did not see him since.

CLEOPATRA   [*to Alexas*] See where he is, who's with him, what he
does.

I did not send you.[6] If you find him sad,
Say I am dancing; if in mirth, report
That I am sudden sick. Quick, and return.

[Exit Alexas.]

CHARMIAN   Madam, methinks if you did love him dearly,
You do not hold the method to enforce
The like from him.

CLEOPATRA   What should I do I do not?

CHARMIAN   In each thing give him way; cross him in nothing.

CLEOPATRA   Thou teachest like a fool: the way to lose him.

CHARMIAN   Tempt him not so too far; I wish, forbear.
In time we hate that which we often fear.

Antony leaves Cleopatra to attend to urgent matters of state in
Rome. While he is there, he agrees to a suggestion that he cement
the alliance by marrying Octavius Caesar's sister, Octavia. His
down-to-earth follower Enobarbus comments to his fellow
warriors, cynically but accurately, that Antony will nonetheless
leave to go "to his Egyptian dish again". He follows this remark
by describing the first meeting between Cleopatra and Antony, in
some of Shakespeare's most evocative verse.

ACT 2, SCENE 2

MAECENAS   She's a most triumphant lady, if report be square to
her.

ENOBARBUS   When she first met Mark Antony, she pursed up his
heart upon the river of Cydnus.

AGRIPPA   There she appeared indeed! Or my reporter devised
well for her.

ENOBARBUS   I will tell you.
The barge she sat in, like a burnished[7] throne,
Burned on the water; the poop[8] was beaten gold;

Purple the sails, and so perfumèd that
The winds were love-sick with them; the oars were
    silver,
Which to the tune of flutes kept stroke, and made
The water which they beat to follow faster,
As amorous of their strokes.[9] For her own person,
It beggared all description: she did lie
In her pavilion, cloth-of-gold of tissue,[10]
O'erpicturing that Venus where we see
The fancy outwork nature.[11] On each side her
Stood pretty dimpled boys, like smiling cupids,
With divers-coloured fans, whose wind did seem
To glow the delicate cheeks which they did cool,
And what they undid did.[12]

AGRIPPA   O, rare for Antony!

ENOBARBUS   Her gentlewomen, like the Nereides,[13]
So many mermaids, tended her i'th' eyes,
And made their bends adornings.[14] At the helm
A seeming mermaid steers. The silken tackle
Swell with the touches of those flower-soft hands
That yarely[15] frame the office. From the barge
A strange invisible perfume hits the sense
Of the adjacent wharfs. The city cast
Her people out upon her, and Antony,
Enthroned i'th' market-place, did sit alone,
Whistling to th'air, which, but for vacancy,[16]
Had gone to gaze on Cleopatra too,
And made a gap in nature.

AGRIPPA   Rare Egyptian!

ENOBARBUS   Upon her landing, Antony sent to her,
Invited her to supper. She replied
It should be better he became her guest,

Which she entreated. Our courteous Antony,

Whom ne'er the word of "No" woman heard speak,

Being barbered ten times o'er, goes to the feast,

And, for his ordinary,[17] pays his heart

For what his eyes eat only.

AGRIPPA   Royal wench!

She made great Caesar lay his sword to bed.

He ploughed her, and she cropped.[18]

ENOBARBUS   I saw her once

Hop forty paces through the public street

And, having lost her breath, she spoke and panted,

That she did make defect perfection,[19]

And, breathless, power breathe forth.

MAECENAS   Now Antony must leave her utterly.

ENOBARBUS   Never! He will not.

Age cannot wither her, nor custom stale

Her infinite variety. Other women cloy

The appetites they feed, but she makes hungry

Where most she satisfies; for vilest things

Become themselves[20] in her, that the holy priests

Bless her when she is riggish.[21]

Back in Egypt, Cleopatra restlessly waits for news, unaware that Antony has married Octavia. Like the scene where Juliet waits for Romeo to come to her after Tybalt's death, the irony of the situation heightens our sense of the lover's longing. Like Orsino, in *Twelfth Night*, Cleopatra calls for music to express her melancholy – then dismisses it.

ACT 2, SCENE 5

    Enter Cleopatra, Charmian, Iras, and Alexas.

CLEOPATRA   Give me some music—music, moody food

Of us that trade in love.

ALL   The music, ho!

Enter Mardian the Eunuch.

CLEOPATRA   Let it alone.

Let's to billiards. Come, Charmian.

CHARMIAN   My arm is sore. Best play with Mardian.

CLEOPATRA   As well a woman with an eunuch played

As with a woman. Come, you'll play with me, sir?

MARDIAN   As well as I can, madam.

CLEOPATRA   And when good will is showed, though't come too
short,

The actor may plead pardon. I'll none now.

Give me mine angle;²² we'll to th' river. There,

My music playing far off, I will betray

Tawny-finned fishes. My bended hook shall pierce

Their slimy jaws, and as I draw them up

I'll think them every one an Antony,

And say "Ah ha! You're caught."

CHARMIAN   'Twas merry when

You wagered on your angling; when your diver

Did hang a salt fish on his hook, which he

With fervency drew up.

CLEOPATRA   That time—O times!—

I laughed him out of patience, and that night

I laughed him into patience; and next morn,

Ere the ninth hour, I drunk him to his bed,

Then put my tires and mantles²³ on him, whilst

I wore his sword Philippan.

After the fatal, off-stage, battle of Actium, where Antony deserts his men to follow Cleopatra's "fearful sails", Cleopatra welcomes a messenger from Caesar more warmly than Antony likes, and they quarrel; in a final, extreme version of her contrary nature, Cleopatra orders her servant to report her death. Antony chooses to commit suicide, to be a "bridegroom" in his death and "run into't / As to a lover's bed." He falls on his sword, but does not immediately die; his men find him, and bring him to the monument where Cleopatra has taken refuge. As he dies, he offers no recriminations, but thinks back to his own high moments and gives Cleopatra advice on how to proceed with Caesar.

ACT 4, SCENE 15

Cleopatra in the monument, above. Enter, below,
Antony, borne by the guard.

CLEOPATRA   O sun,

Burn the great sphere thou mov'st in![24] Darkling[25]
   stand
The varying shore o'th' world. O Antony,
Antony, Antony! Help, Charmian; help, Iras, help!
Help, friends below! Let's draw him hither.

ANTONY   Peace!
Not Caesar's valour hath o'erthrown Antony,
But Antony's hath triumphed on itself.

CLEOPATRA   So it should be that none but Antony
Should conquer Antony; but woe 'tis so.

ANTONY   I am dying, Egypt, dying; only
I here importune[26] death awhile, until
Of many thousand kisses the poor last

I lay upon thy lips.

CLEOPATRA   I dare not,[27] dear.

Dear my lord, pardon. I dare not

Lest I be taken. Not th'imperious[28] show

Of the full-fortuned Caesar ever shall

Be brooched[29] with me. If knife, drugs, serpents, have

Edge, sting, or operation, I am safe.

Your wife Octavia, with her modest eyes

And still conclusion,[30] shall acquire no honour

Demuring[31] upon me. But come, come, Antony—

Help me, my women—we must draw thee up.

Assist, good friends.

     [*They begin lifting.*]

ANTONY   Oh, quick, or I am gone.

CLEOPATRA Here's sport indeed! How heavy weighs my lord!

Our strength is all gone into heaviness;[32]

That makes the weight. Had I great Juno's power,

The strong-winged Mercury should fetch thee up

And set thee by Jove's side.[33] Yet come a little.

Wishers were ever fools. O come, come, come,

     [*They heave Antony aloft to Cleopatra.*]

And welcome, welcome! Die where thou hast lived;

Quicken[34] with kissing. Had my lips that power,

Thus would I wear them out.

ALL   A heavy sight!

ANTONY I am dying, Egypt, dying.

Give me some wine and let me speak a little—

CLEOPATRA No, let me speak, and let me rail so high

That the false huswife[35] Fortune break her wheel,

Provoked by my offence.

ANTONY   One word, sweet queen:

Of Caesar seek your honour with your safety.
                    Oh!

CLEOPATRA   They do not go together.

ANTONY   Gentle, hear me.
            None about Caesar trust but Proculeius.

CLEOPATRA   My resolution and my hands I'll trust;
            None about Caesar.

ANTONY   The miserable change now at my end,
            Lament nor sorrow at, but please your thoughts
            In feeding them with those my former fortunes
            Wherein I lived the greatest prince o'th' world,
            The noblest; and do now not basely die,
            Not cowardly put off my helmet to
            My countryman; a Roman by a Roman
            Valiantly vanquished. Now my spirit is going,
            I can no more.

CLEOPATRA   Noblest of men, woo't ³⁶die?
            Hast thou no care of me? Shall I abide
            In this dull world, which in thy absence is
            No better than a sty? Oh, see, my women,
            The crown o'th' earth doth melt. [*Antony dies.*] My
                lord!
            Oh, withered is the garland of the war,
            The soldier's pole³⁷ is fallen: young boys and girls
            Are level now with men. The odds³⁸ is gone,
            And there is nothing left remarkable
            Beneath the visiting moon. [*She faints.*]

CHARMIAN   Oh, quietness, lady!

IRAS   She's dead too, our sovereign.

CHARMIAN   Lady!

IRAS   Madam!

CHARMIAN   O madam, madam, madam!

IRAS	Royal Egypt, Empress!
	[*Cleopatra stirs.*]
CHARMIAN	Peace, peace, Iras.
CLEOPATRA	No more but e'en a woman, and commanded

By such poor passion as the maid that milks
And does the meanest chores. It were for me
To throw my sceptre at the injurious gods
To tell them that this world did equal theirs
Till they had stolen our jewel. All's but naught;
Patience is sottish,[39] and impatience does
Become a dog that's mad. Then is it sin
To rush into the secret house of death
Ere death dare come to us? How do you, women?
What, what, good cheer! Why, how now,
    Charmian?
My noble girls! Ah, women, women, look;
Our lamp is spent, it's out. Good sirs, take heart.
We'll bury him, and then what's brave, what's
    noble,
Let's do't[40] after the high Roman fashion
And make death proud to take us. Come, away.
This case[41] of that huge spirit now is cold.
Ah, women, women! Come, we have no friend
But resolution and the briefest end.

               Exeunt, bearing off Antony's body.

Thus, in Antony's death, Cleopatra discovers that as well as queen she is simply a woman who has lost her love. In due course she is betrayed to Caesar by the very person – Proculeius – whom Antony recommended she trust. She puts her backup plan into effect as a country "clown" brings her poisonous asps, hidden under a basket of figs. Her women dress her as she prepares to greet Antony in death.

ACT 5, SCENE 2

CLEOPATRA Give me my robe. Put on my crown. I have
Immortal longings in me. Now no more
The juice of Egypt's grape shall moist this lip.
  [*The women dress her.*]
Yare, yare,[42] good Iras! quick! Methinks I hear
Antony call. I see him rouse himself
To praise my noble act. I hear him mock
The luck of Caesar, which the gods give men
To excuse their after wrath.[43] Husband, I come.
Now to that name my courage prove my title![44]
I am fire and air; my other elements[45]
I give to baser life. So, have you done?
Come then, and take the last warmth of my lips.
Farewell, kind Charmian. Iras, long farewell.
  [*Kisses them. Iras falls and dies.*]
Have I the aspic[46] in my lips? Dost fall?
If thou and nature can so gently part,
The stroke of death is as a lover's pinch,
Which hurts and is desired. Dost thou lie still?
If thus thou vanishest,[47] thou tell'st the world
It is not worth leave-taking.

CHARMIAN Dissolve, thick cloud, and rain, that I may say
The gods themselves do weep.

CLEOPATRA   This proves me base.
If she first meet the curlèd Antony,[48]
He'll make demand of her, and spend that kiss
Which is my heaven to have.
  [*To an asp, which she applies to her breast*]
                                          Come, thou mortal wretch,
With thy sharp teeth this knot intrinsicate[49]
Of life at once untie. Poor venomous fool,

	Be angry and dispatch. Oh, couldst thou speak,
	That I might hear thee call great Caesar ass
	Unpolicied![50]
CHARMIAN	O eastern star!
CLEOPATRA	Peace, peace!
	Dost thou not see my baby[51] at my breast
	That sucks the nurse asleep?
CHARMIAN	Oh, break! Oh, break!
CLEOPATRA	As sweet as balm, as soft as air, as gentle—
	O Antony! Nay, I will take thee too.
	[applying another asp to her arm]
	What should I stay— *dies.*
CHARMIAN	In this vile world! So fare thee well.
	Now boast thee, Death, in thy possession lies
	A lass unparalleled. Downy windows,[52] close,
	And golden Phoebus,[53] never be beheld
	Of eyes again so royal! Your crown's awry;
	I'll mend it, and then play—
	Enter the Guard, rustling in.
GUARD	Where's the Queen?
CHARMIAN	Speak softly. Wake her not.
GUARD	Caesar hath sent—
CHARMIAN	Too slow a messenger.

The Winter's Tale

Antony and Cleopatra ends tragically, but without the agonizingly bad luck that characterizes the end of *Romeo and Juliet*; Cleopatra will be buried beside Antony, and, in Caesar's words, "no grave upon the earth / Shall clip in it a pair so famous".

In his last plays, Shakespeare moves away from the tragic mode toward a genre now known as "romance", where potentially tragic forces are, in the end, mitigated, often through supernatural forces. On their own, humans are still unable to ensure that the course of true love runs smooth; there is no magic love-potion in these plays, but there is magic (especially in *The Tempest*), and the gods intervene in *Pericles* and *Cymbeline* to ensure that humans figure things out as they should. *The Winter's Tale* involves two such interventions: an oracle, and something that seems very much like magic. As the name of the play implies, Shakespeare chooses to work with a plot that is as fantastic as the stories told around the fire on a winter's night.

The play begins with Polixenes, King of Bohemia, visiting his childhood friend Leontes, King of Sicilia. Polixenes decides that it is time to return and Leontes tries to persuade him to stay; he fails in his plea and asks his pregnant wife, Hermione, to plead on his behalf. She does so, successfully – with disastrous results.

ACT 1, SCENE 2

LEONTES	Is he won yet?
HERMIONE	He'll stay, my lord.
LEONTES	At my request he would not.
	Hermione, my dearest, thou never spok'st
	To better purpose.

HERMIONE	Never?
LEONTES	Never but once.
HERMIONE	What! Have I twice said well? When was't before?

I prithee tell me; cram's with praise, and make's

As fat as tame things. One good deed dying
    tongueless

Slaughters a thousand waiting upon that.[1]

Our praises are our wages; you may ride's

With one soft kiss a thousand furlongs[2] ere

With spur we heat[3] an acre. But to th' goal:

My last good deed was to entreat his stay;

What was my first? It has an elder sister,

Or I mistake you. Oh, would her name were Grace!

But once before I spoke to th' purpose—When?

Nay, let me have't; I long.

LEONTES	Why, that was when

Three crabbèd months had soured themselves
    to death,

Ere I could make thee open thy white hand

And clap[4] thyself my love; then didst thou utter

"I am yours for ever."

HERMIONE	'Tis Grace indeed.

Why, lo you now, I have spoke to th' purpose twice:

The one for ever earned a royal husband;

Th'other for some while a friend.

    [*giving her hand to Polixenes*]

LEONTES	[*aside*] Too hot, too hot!

To mingle friendship far is mingling bloods.[5]

I have tremor cordis[6] on me; my heart dances,

But not for joy, not joy. This entertainment

May a free face[7] put on, derive a liberty

From heartiness, from bounty, fertile bosom,[8]

And well become the agent[9]—'t may, I grant;
But to be paddling palms and pinching fingers,
As now they are, and making practised smiles
As in a looking-glass; and then to sigh, as 'twere
The mort o' th' deer[10]—oh, that is entertainment
My bosom likes not, nor my brows.[11]

Leontes' jealousy seems to come from nowhere – he needs no
Iago to tempt him. He immediately decides that he will arrange
for his trusted follower Camillo to poison Polixenes. He tries to
persuade Camillo that his suspicions are justified; but his language
is obsessive, his syntax fractured, as Shakespeare creates an intensity
of image and rhythm that bombards Camillo.

LEONTES   Ha' not you seen, Camillo—
        But that's past doubt you have, or your eye-glass[12]
        Is thicker than a cuckold's horn[13]—or heard—
        For to a vision so apparent[14] rumour
        Cannot be mute—or thought—for cogitation
        Resides not in that man that does not think—
        My wife is slippery? If thou wilt confess,
        Or else be impudently negative,
        To have nor eyes, nor ears, nor thought,[15] then say
        My wife's a hobby-horse,[16] deserves a name
        As rank as any flax-wench[17] that puts to
        Before her troth-plight.[18] Say't and justify't.
CAMILLO   I would not be a stander-by to hear
        My sovereign mistress clouded so, without
        My present vengeance taken; 'shrew[19] my heart,
        You never spoke what did become you less
        Than this; which to reiterate were sin
        As deep as that, though true.

LEONTES   Is whispering nothing?
Is leaning cheek to cheek? Is meeting noses?
Kissing with inside lip? Stopping the career
Of laughter with a sigh (a note infallible
Of breaking honesty)? Horsing foot on foot?[20]
Skulking in corners? Wishing clocks more swift,[21]
Hours, minutes, noon, midnight? And all eyes
Blind with the pin and web[22] but theirs, theirs only,
That would unseen be wicked. Is this nothing?
Why, then the world and all that's in't is nothing,
The covering sky is nothing, Bohemia nothing,
My wife is nothing, nor nothing have these nothings,
If this be nothing.

Events move rapidly: Camillo defects and escapes with Polixenes. Leontes accuses Hermione, who defends herself with dignity; he imprisons her whereupon she gives birth to their second child, a girl. The splendid Paulina, supporter of Hermione, brings the baby to her father, but he disowns his baby daughter and insists that she be abandoned on the sea-coast of Polixenes' kingdom, Bohemia.[23] Hermione is brought to trial, where Leontes hears from the oracle that she is blameless, and that "the king shall live without an heir, if that which is lost, be not found". Hermione faints, and is carried off. We hear from Paulina that both she and her first-born son have died. Leontes, not altogether surprisingly, realizes the error of his judgement. The baby daughter, Perdita, is indeed abandoned on the sea-coast of Bohemia by Paulina's husband who (in Shakespeare's most striking stage direction) exits, "pursued by a bear" and is eaten (offstage).

Sixteen years pass. Polixenes' son, Florizel, falls in love with a shepherd girl he meets while hunting; and of course, this being a winter's tale, it is Leontes' abandoned daughter, Perdita. Suspecting

his son of consorting with a mere shepherdess, Polixenes disguises himself and brings Camillo with him to see what is going on. They find Florizel and Perdita in the middle of a harvest feast, where she (like a saner version of Ophelia) distributes appropriate flowers to those who stand by.

ACT 4, SCENE 4

PERDITA.   [*to Polixenes and Camillo in disguise*] Here's flowers
        for you:
    Hot lavender, mints, savory, marjoram,
    The marigold, that goes to bed wi'th' sun
    And with him rises, weeping; these are flowers
    Of middle summer, and I think they are given
    To men of middle age. You're very welcome.

CAMILLO   I should leave grazing, were I of your flock,
    And only live by gazing.

PERDITA   Out, alas!
    You'd be so lean that blasts of January
    Would blow you through and through. [*to Florizel*]
        Now, my fair'st friend,
    I would I had some flowers o'th' spring, that might
    Become your time of day—and yours, and yours,
        [*to Mopsa and the other girls*]
    That wear upon your virgin branches yet
    Your maidenheads growing. O Proserpina,[24]
    For the flowers now that, frighted, thou let'st fall
    From Dis's waggon! Daffodils,
    That come before the swallow dares, and take
    The winds of March with beauty; violets, dim,
    But sweeter than the lids of Juno's eyes
    Or Cytherea's[25] breath; pale primroses,
    That die unmarried ere they can behold

Bright Phoebus[26] in his strength (a malady
Most incident to maids);[27] bold oxlips, and
The crown imperial;[28] lilies of all kinds,
The flower-de-luce being one. O, these I lack
To make you garlands of; and my sweet friend
To strew him o'er and o'er!

FLORIZEL   What, like a corpse?

PERDITA   No, like a bank for love to lie and play on;
Not like a corpse; or if—not to be buried,
But quick,[29] and in mine arms. Come, take your
    flowers.
Methinks I play as I have seen them do
In Whitsun pastorals.[30] Sure this robe of mine
Does change my disposition.

FLORIZEL   What you do
Still betters what is done. When you speak, sweet,
I'd have you do it ever. When you sing,
I'd have you buy and sell so, so give alms,
Pray so, and, for the ord'ring your affairs,
To sing them too. When you do dance, I wish you
A wave o'th' sea, that you might ever do
Nothing but that; move still, still so,
And own[31] no other function. Each your doing,
So singular in each particular,[32]
Crowns what you are doing in the present deeds,[33]
That all your acts are queens.

PERDITA   O Doricles,[34]
Your praises are too large.[35] But that your youth,
And the true blood which peeps fairly through't,
Do plainly give you out an unstained[36] shepherd,
With wisdom I might fear, my Doricles,
You wooed me the false way.[37]

FLORIZEL	I think you have
	As little skill to fear as I have purpose
	To put you to't. But come; our dance, I pray.
	Your hand, my Perdita; so turtles[38] pair
	That never mean to part.
PERDITA	I'll swear for 'em.
POLIXENES	This is the prettiest low-born lass that ever
	Ran on the green-sward;[39] nothing she does or seems
	But smacks of something greater than herself,
	Too noble for this place.
CAMILLO	He tells her something
	That makes her blood look out.[40] Good sooth, she is
	The queen of curds and cream.

Polixenes unmasks, and demands that his son reject Perdita. The young lovers decide to flee, and with Camillo's help they return to Sicilia, where Perdita is revealed to be Leontes' daughter through some of her belongings (I am skipping some really good details here, especially the brilliant part played by the rogue Autolycus). Polixenes arrives in pursuit of his son, and all are reconciled.

Finally, in another rare surprise ending, Paulina takes them all to see a statue of Hermione by the great sculptor Giulio Romano. As he looks at the statue, Leontes realizes that the human warmth of Hermione was far to be preferred to the cold stone of the statue.

ACT 5, SCENE 3

PAULINA	Prepare
	To see the life as lively mocked[41] as ever
	Still sleep mocked death. Behold; and say 'tis well.
	[*Paulina draws a curtain, and discovers Hermione*
	standing like a statue.]
	I like your silence; it the more shows off

Your wonder; but yet speak. First, you, my liege.
Comes it not something near?

LEONTES   Her natural posture!
Chide me, dear stone, that I may say indeed
Thou art Hermione; or rather, thou art she
In thy not chiding; for she was as tender
As infancy and grace. But yet, Paulina,
Hermione was not so much wrinkled, nothing
So aged as this seems.

POLIXENES   O, not by much.

PAULINA   So much the more our carver's excellence,
Which lets go by some sixteen years and makes her
As[42] she lived now.

LEONTES   As now she might have done,
So much to my good comfort as it is
Now piercing to my soul. O, thus she stood,
Even with such life of majesty—warm life,
As now it coldly stands—when first I wooed her.
I am ashamed. Does not the stone rebuke me
For being more stone than it? O royal piece,[43]
There's magic in thy majesty, which has
My evils conjured[44] to remembrance, and
From thy admiring daughter took the spirits,[45]
Standing like stone with thee.

PERDITA   And give me leave,
And do not say 'tis superstition that
I kneel, and then implore her blessing. Lady,
Dear queen, that ended when I but began,
Give me that hand of yours to kiss.

PAULINA   Oh, patience!
The statue is but newly fixed, the colour's
Not dry.

LEONTES	The fixture of her eye has motion in't,
	As[46] we are mocked with art.
PAULINA	I'll draw the curtain.
	My lord's almost so far transported that
	He'll think anon it lives.
LEONTES	O sweet Paulina,
	Make me to think so twenty years together!
	No settled senses of the world can match
	The pleasure of that madness. Let't alone.
PAULINA	I am sorry, sir, I have thus far stirred you; but
	I could afflict you farther.
LEONTES	Do, Paulina;
	For this affliction has a taste as sweet
	As any cordial[47] comfort. Still, methinks,
	There is an air comes from her. What fine chisel
	Could ever yet cut breath? Let no man mock me,
	For I will kiss her.
PAULINA	Good my lord, forbear.
	The ruddiness upon her lip is wet;
	You'll mar it if you kiss it, stain your own
	With oily painting. Shall I draw the curtain?
LEONTES	No, not these twenty years.
PERDITA	So long could I
	Stand by, a looker-on.
PAULINA	Either forbear,
	Quit presently the chapel, or resolve you
	For more amazement. If you can behold it,
	I'll make the statue move indeed, descend,
	And take you by the hand—but then you'll think,
	Which I protest against, I am assisted
	By wicked powers.

LEONTES   What you can make her do
          I am content to look on; what to speak
          I am content to hear; for 'tis as easy
          To make her speak as move.

PAULINA   It is required
          You do awake your faith. Then all stand still;
          Or those that think it is unlawful business
          I am about, let them depart.

LEONTES   Proceed.
          No foot shall stir.

PAULINA   Music, awake her: strike.[48] [*music*]
          'Tis time; descend; be stone no more; approach;
          Strike all that look upon with marvel. Come;
          I'll fill your grave up. Stir; nay, come away.
          Bequeath to death your numbness, for from him[49]
          Dear life redeems you. You perceive she stirs.

[*Hermione comes down from the pedestal.*]

Start not; her actions shall be holy as

You hear my spell is lawful. [*to Leontes*] Do not shun

    her[50]

Until you see her die again; for then

You kill her double. Nay, present your hand.

When she was young you wooed her; now, in age,

Is she become the suitor?

LEONTES   O, she's warm!

If this be magic, let it be an art

Lawful as eating.

POLIXENES   She embraces him.

CAMILLO   She hangs about his neck.

If she pertain to life,[51] let her speak too.

POLIXENES   Ay, and make it manifest where she has lived,

Or how stolen from the dead.

PAULINA   That she is living,

Were it but told you, should be hooted at

Like an old tale; but it appears she lives,

Though yet she speak not. Mark a little while.

[*to Perdita*] Please you to interpose, fair madam.

    Kneel,

And pray your mother's blessing. [*to Hermione*]

    Turn, good lady;

Our Perdita is found.

HERMIONE   You gods, look down,

And from your sacred vials[52] pour your graces

Upon my daughter's head! Tell me, mine own,

Where hast thou been preserved? Where lived? How

    found

Thy father's court? For thou shalt hear that I,

Knowing by Paulina that the Oracle

	Gave hope thou wast in being, have preserved
	Myself to see the issue.
PAULINA	There's time enough for that,
	Lest they desire upon this push[53] to trouble
	Your joys with like relation. Go together,
	You precious winners all; your exultation
	Partake to every one. I, an old turtle,
	Will wing me to some withered bough, and there
	My mate, that's never to be found again,
	Lament till I am lost.
LEONTES	Oh, peace, Paulina!
	Thou shouldst a husband take by my consent,
	As I by thine a wife. This is a match,
	And made between's by vows. Thou hast found mine;
	But how, is to be questioned; for I saw her,
	As I thought, dead; and have in vain said many
	A prayer upon her grave.[54] I'll not seek far—
	For him, I partly know his mind—to find thee
	An honourable husband. Come, Camillo,
	And take her by the hand, whose worth and honesty
	Is richly noted, and here justified
	By us, a pair of kings.

In a gently implausible ending, not only is Hermione discovered to be alive, but Paulina acquires a second husband. Before revealing that Hermione is alive (or bringing her back to life), Paulina requires that the onlookers awaken their faith; in the troubled real world of human love, and in the likely absence of oracles and love-potions, perhaps the best hope is in mutual trust, and in a passion that is neither too hot nor too cold.

Endnotes

INTRODUCTION

1 Marc Norman and Tom Stoppard, *Shakespeare in Love*. London: Faber and Faber, 1999, pp. 94, 148.
2 See Mary Beth Rose, *The Expense of Spirit*, p.17. For the ecclesiastical courts, see Martin Ingram, *Church Court* and F.G. Emmison, *Elizabethan Life*.
3 Lawrence Stone, *The Family*, p.135.
4 Ingram, p.142.
5 See Peter Laslett, *Household and Family in Past Time*. The average age of marriage in the period 1566–1619 was twenty-seven, with men being slightly older than women.
6 Emilia's powerful words recall the closely similar sentiments spoken by Shylock as he claims common humanity with others: "Hath not a Jew eyes? Hath not a Jew hands, organs, dimensions, senses, affections, passions, fed with the same food, hurt with the same weapons, subject to the same diseases, healed by the same means, warmed and cooled by the same winter and summer, as a Christian is? If you prick us, do we not bleed? If you tickle us, do we not laugh?" (*The Merchant of Venice*, 3.1.56–63.)
7 In awe.
8 *The Book of the Courtier*. Trans. Sir Thomas Hoby (Everyman Library. London: Dent, 1928). Castiglione followed and adapted Platonic philosophy throughout his work.
9 Bitterness.
10 Calumny is slander.
11 See Rogers, *The Troublesome Helpmate*.
12 Edward Berry has argued that the attitudes to hawking in the period make his actions less repugnant than might seem the case, since the hawk was treated with great respect by its trainers. See *Shakespeare and the Hunt*, Chapter 4.
13 We may be tempted to see in this an echo of Shakespeare's own early marriage.

SONNETS
Introduction:

1 Readers curious to know more about the long history of candidates for the position of the young friend will find ample references in the Further Reading.
2 John Kerrigan, one of the finest editors of the *Sonnets*, describes the relationship between Shakespeare and the persona of the sonnets admirably: "The text is neither fictive nor confessional. Shakespeare stands behind the first person of his sequence . . . sometimes near the poetic 'I', sometimes farther off, but never without some degree of rhetorical projection." (p.11).
3 Heather Dubrow, in "Incertainties", p.113. Shakespeare may have been writing for his "private friends", as a reference by Frances Meres in 1598 suggests.
4 *Homosexual Desire*, p.136.
5 Several critics have attempted to reorder the sonnets to create more coherent, or simply different, narratives. There is, however, no agreement on any of these suggested reorderings.

1: 1 The first seventeen sonnets argue that the youth should marry and have children in order to preserve his physical beauty through children.
    2 Procreation, offspring.
    3 The elder, the parent.
    4 Betrothed.
    5 From your own substance.
    6 (i) contents, (ii) contentment.
    7 Paradoxically, wasting by saving (himself from marriage).
    8 To devour the offspring the world deserves, by choosing a childless death.

2: 1 Create wrinkles in his brow.
    2 Attractive clothes (and, metaphorically, youthful flesh).
    3 Investment.
    4 Justify my accounting, and excuse my age.
    5 Through inheritance.

3: 1 Mirror.
    2 Youthful state.
    3 Cheat.
    4 Unploughed.
    5 Farming (punningly).
    6 When you look back in your old age.

4: 1 The extended financial image here is of a spendthrift, failing to return Nature's bounty.
    2 Generous.
    3 Previously a spendthrift, the youth is now a miser, failing to pass on his wealth of beauty.
    4 Commerce.

5: 1 The following two sonnets can be read as a single poem, as the second expands further on the image of flowers distilled for their perfume as a figure for greater permanence in beauty.
    2 The passage of time.
    3 Make ugly.
    4 Destroys.
    5 Distilled perfume.
    6 Held captive.

6: 1 Container – metaphorically for the womb.
    2 Laws against usury (lending money for interest) in the period were strict, though frequently ignored.

7: 1 East.
    2 The sun.
    3 Every earthly eye.
    4 Paying respects.
    5 Having risen to a peak at noon.

8: 1 (You) whom it is music to hear.
    2 The paradox is that the youth is sombre while listening to sweet sounds, instead of rejoicing in them.
    3 The youth defeats the possibility of harmony (musical parts) by remaining a single, unaccompanied tune.
    4 Sympathetic vibration: one string vibrating when another tuned to the same pitch is sounded.
    5 Again the paradox of harmony is that it is one sound made up of many.

9: 1 Childless.
    2 Continually.
    3 Separate, individual.
    4 The economic argument, very modern, is that one person's spending stimulates the economy for others.

10: 1 Scruple.
     2 His body; the metaphor is of an estate.

11: 1 Sixty years would mean the end of civilization if there were no children born to carry on.
     2 A stamp used to create multiple impressions or images.

12: 1 Splendid.
     2 Black.
     3 Earlier.
     4 Bound.
     5 Metaphorically for the hay cart.
     6 The bristles of the sheaves of wheat or barley, suggestive of an old man's beard.
     7 Except for having children.
     8 Defy.

13: 1 On Earth.
     2 Termination, end.
     3 Thriftiness (punningly).

14:	1	Foretell my conclusions.
	2	Famines.
	3	Forecast to the last minute.
	4	Appointing.
	5	Frequent prediction.
	6	Abundance (children).
15:	1	For the first time, the writer suggests that his art might provide an alternative immortality; a proposition denied in the second of this group of two sonnets.
	2	The Earth.
	3	Encouraged and held back.
	4	Handsome.
	5	Thought.
	6	Consults, competes.
16:	1	Infertile.
	2	Unplanted, without seeds.
	3	Portrait (in verse).
	4	Skill in lovemaking.
17:	1	Verses.
	2	More talkative than truthful.
	3	Exaggerated lines (literally rhythm).
18:	1	The hesitancy in suggesting immortality through verse of the last two sonnets is discarded in this famous and triumphant sonnet.
	2	The time available in summer.
	3	The sun.
	4	Everything beautiful declines eventually from that state of beauty.
	5	By bad luck, or by the natural passage of time.
19:	1	A mythical, long-lived bird that was supposed to die in fire and be reborn from the ashes (here her blood).
	2	(i) antic or capricious, (ii) old.
	3	Unstained, uninjured.
20:	1	This crucial sonnet creates a wry myth of origin: the youth's beauty is such that Nature fell in love with him, and, since Nature is a woman, she turned him at the last moment into a man. The ambiguous sense of sexuality in the poem is discussed in the introduction to this section.
	2	Natural; compare "painted" in the next sonnet.
	3	Both master and mistress, male and female.
	4	The eye is imagined as giving forth beams that make the objects it sees shine.
	5	A man whose appearance (colour) is superior to all others, male or female.
	6	Naure (a woman) added the one thing – a penis – that is of no use to the Poet.
	7	Marked, with a pun on "prick".
	8	The Poet will have his love, while women will have (treasure) his sexual activity. The pun is again on "use" as an investment; as in Sonnet 129 to the dark woman, orgasm is seen as "spending."
21:	1	Poet.
	2	Artificial.
	3	Compares his loved one to every kind of beauty; compare Sonnet 130 to the dark woman.
	4	Sphere (world).
	5	Stars.
	6	Gossip; what today we would call advertising.
22:	1	Mirror.
	2	So long as you remain youthful.
	3	End.
	4	Your beauty is the decorous clothing of my heart, which is enclosed in your breast, as yours is in mine.
	5	I will care for myself for your sake.
	6	Carefully.
	7	The first warning of imperfect love: the youth should not expect to get his heart back if the writer's heart is "slain" (by loss of love or betrayal).
23:	1	Who gets stage fright.
	2	A wild animal whose fury weakens its heart.

	3	Mistrusting myself.
	4	Possibly the narrative poems *Venus and Adonis* and *The Rape of Lucrece*.
	5	Silent messengers.
24:	1	Engraved upon a tablet.
	2	Lack.
25:	1	Unexpectedly.
	2	Painstaking.
	3	Erased.
26:	1	This poem is often taken as evidence that the youth was an aristocrat, since it can be read as requesting patronage. On the other hand, Shakespeare was good at metaphors.
	2	Allegiance.
	3	Letter.
	4	Good opinions.
	5	Place my poor (naked) verse in your thoughts.
	6	Astrological favour.
	7	Put me to the test.
27:	1	This sonnet and the next form a double sonnet.
	2	The word means "travail" (hard work) as well.
28:	1	The day disturbed by lack of sleep, and sleep by the activities of the day.
	2	Day; the *other* is night.
	3	Dark-coloured.
	4	When the stars do not twinkle, the youth's beauty makes the evening golden.
29:	1	Useless.
	2	With the same (good) looks.
	3	Range (of power or learning).
	4	Most possess.
	5	By chance.
	6	State of mind or fortune.
30:	1	The sittings of a court; in the next line, witnesses are summoned.
	2	Re-hash old woes, lamenting time wasted.
	3	Unused to weeping.
	4	Endless.
	5	Loss.
	6	Retell.
31:	1	Beloved by all.
	2	Qualities.
	3	Mourning.
	4	Memorials.
32:	1	This is the first poem that mentions the possibility of rival poets.
	2	By chance.
	3	Improvements in poetic style.
	4	Greater eloquence.
	5	Better creation (poem).
	6	Better equipped (the metaphor is of an army).
33:	1	These next three sonnets form the arc of a disagreement, where the youth has apparently injured the Poet in some way.
	2	The sun, gold in the morning.
	3	The alchemists sought to convert base metals to gold.
	4	Bank of clouds.
	5	My loved one (the youth).
	6	Of the upper air.
34:	1	Unwholesome vapours.
	2	Medicine; following the image of the salve two lines earlier.
	3	The original reads *loss*.
35:	1	Budworm.
	2	Rationalizing his behaviour through comparison.
	3	Reason.
	4	In the legal sense: defence lawyer. The metaphor continues in the following lines.
36:	1	This sonnet may form the first part of a double sonnet with 39.
	2	Separate (two).
	3	Defects, perhaps of honour.
	4	Attitude.
	5	Effect of creating one sole (soul) person.

	6	Since we are one, your good reputation becomes mine. This couplet is repeated in Sonnet 96.
37:	1	Aged and infirm.
	2	Handicapped.
	3	Given nobility by your qualities.
	4	Abundance.
	5	The concept is given reality; Shakespeare is using Platonic terminology.
38:	1	Lack.
	2	Topic, subject.
	3	The creative urge.
	4	In Greek mythology there were nine Muses, daughters of Apollo, god of music and poetry.
	5	Verses.
39:	1	Because of.
	2	Cover, ameliorate.
40:	1	This group of three sonnets suggests that the youth has seduced someone loved by the writer, possibly the dark woman; the poems are almost masochistic in their rationalization of the youth's behaviour.
	2	Playing on the love the writer feels for the youth, and the Poet's mistress, or lover.
	3	You use my loved one sexually.
	4	It is harder to accept injury from someone we love than from someone we hate.
	5	An extraordinary oxymoron. See the Introduction to this section, p.29.
41:	1	Licentiousness.
	2	The original reads *he*; possibly it means that no man will leave until he has had sex with such a woman.
	3	Place (here his mistress).
42:	1	Wrong.
	2	Test; try her out sexually.
43:	1	The following three sonnets can be read as a triple sonnet; they all explore absence from the loved one.
	2	Sleep.
	3	Of no interest.
	4	In the darkness of night; directed toward the brightness of the loved one.
	5	Thou whose shadowy dream-self makes bright the shadows of night.
	6	Again, his dream-self.
44:	1	Heavy matter (the elements of earth and water, referred to later in the sonnet).
	2	Wait for time to move in a leisurely fashion.
45:	1	The other two elements, (light) air and fire.
	2	The paradox is explained in the following lines.
	3	The elements each represented a characteristic personality; melancholy was associated with earth and winter, hence with death.
	4	The ideal was a balance between the four elements
46:	1	The next two sonnets form a pair exploring the duality of eye and heart.
	2	The syntax is inverted: the eye would bar the sight of the loved one from the heart.
	3	The eye; the metaphor of a trial continues in the following lines where thoughts are *empanelled* as a jury.
	4	Decide.
	5	Share (literally, half).
47:	1	Pact.
	2	I am always with my thoughts.
48:	1	Strongest.
	2	Prison cells.
	3	Come and go.
49:	1	In preparation for.
	2	Made a final accounting; the metaphor continues in the next line.
	3	Careful thoughts.
	4	Find rationalizations (something Shakespeare's dramatic lovers are very good at).

	5	Fortify.
	6	Merit.
50:	1	The next two sonnets explore similar imagery as the writer travels away from the object of his love.
	2	Sadly.
51:	1	Haste.
	2	An extreme of speed.
	3	The original reads *neigh*, which makes a kind of sense.
	4	An old horse.
52:	1	To avoid.
	2	Or principal jewels in the necklace.
	3	(i) holds you, (ii) watches over you.
53:	1	Shades of the past: the mythical figures mentioned later in the poem.
	2	Here the literal shadow cast by the sun.
	3	See the selections from *Venus and Adonis* below.
	4	Helen of Troy, whose fabled beauty instigated the Trojan war. The writer uses both masculine (Adonis) and feminine ideals of beauty to describe the youth.
	5	Abundance, harvest.
54:	1	The dog rose, which has little scent.
	2	Unnoticed.
	3	By distillation.
	4	Fade, die.
	5	The original reads *by*.
55:	1	Stone grave markers (on the floor of a church).
	2	Wars, battles.
	3	God of war.
	4	Enmity, that brings forgetfulness.
56:	1	Let not love's urge be less keen than physical appetite.
	2	Until eyes close with satiety.
	3	Two newly engaged lovers.
57:	1	This and the next sonnet explore the image of the writer's slavish acceptance of the youth's behaviours; they are so similar that they may be reworkings of the same sonnet rather than the kind of pair we find elsewhere.
	2	Attend.
	3	Seemingly endless.
	4	In your desire. *Will* is capitalized in the original version, emphasizing the pun on Shakespeare's name.
58:	1	That I should even think of controlling.
	2	Await.
	3	Let me suffer the effect of your absence, while you are free (and behaving with *liberty*, licentiousness).
	4	Patiently suffer each rebuke you offer.
	5	Wish.
	6	Privilege.
59:	1	Deceived.
	2	Trying to be original.
	3	Historical record.
	4	Since thoughts were first expressed in writing.
	5	Whether we are superior.
	6	The revolving of the sun; what goes around, comes around.
60:	1	In sequence, all struggle forward.
	2	The new-born child.
	3	The submerged metaphor here is of the span of human life compared to the sun moving across the sky.
	4	Pierce through; destroy.
	5	Wrinkles.
61:	1	Direction.
62:	1	Battered.
	2	Weather-beaten old age.
63:	1	In preparation for the time when.
	2	Also with the sense *travailed*, laboured.
	3	Steeply descending (toward death).
64:	1	The next two form a powerful double sonnet on the ravages of time and the fragility of love.

2 Evil, destructive.
3 Costly aged monuments.
4 Brass memorial plaques (torn down during the dissolution of the monasteries).
5 The coastline of England had changed within living memory.
6 Increasing abundance with famine, and *vice versa*.

65: 1 This one line summarizes the previous sonnet.
2 Solemn destruction.
3 The metaphor is of besieging a castle with a battering ram.
4 Where shall the youth (Time's jewel) be hidden from the coffin (Time's chest)?

66: 1 The list that follows.
2 The deserving person.
3 Worthlessness.
4 Betrayed.
5 Ineffective leadership.
6 With the authority of a teacher.
7 Foolishness.
8 Good waits on evil (its captain).

67: 1 This, and the next sonnet, explore a conflict between art and nature in the expression of beauty.
2 Why.
3 The kinds of ills listed in the previous sonnet; these two may form a double sonnet.
4 Sin will gain advantage by his presence.
5 Adorn.
6 Inferior beauty seeks false (shadow) roses (in its cheeks).
7 Treasury (Nature has spent all on the youth).
8 Preserves.
9 The writer looks back to "the good old days" as being superior.

68: 1 Artificial looks (makeup).
2 Hair from those who had died was used to make wigs for the living.
3 Tombs.
4 Again, the ideal earlier days.

69: 1 Lack.
2 Even enemies have to admit the truth of the youth's beauty.
3 Exterior beauty.
4 Contradict.
5 They judge your mind through your actions.
6 Blemish.
7 Cheap, too available (like a weed).

70: 1 Slander always targets the beautiful.
2 So long as you are virtuous, slander makes you more admirable, as time will prove your innocence.
3 Slander is compared to the canker worm.
4 Youth (prime of life).
5 The temptations of youth.
6 Some suspicion of evil.
7 Own.

71: 1 In the next two sonnets, the writer imagines the effect his death might have on the youth.
2 The tocsin, the church bell that tolls when someone has died.
3 Mingled with earth.
4 Repeat.

72: 1 Require.
2 That your love make you lie in order to speak well of me.
3 Presumably this poem.

73: 1 This most moving sonnet where the writer sees himself on the brink of death is followed by one that attempts to find a positive resolution.
2 Recently.
3 This justly famous line recalls the abbeys that were ruined in the dissolution of the monasteries under Henry VIII.
4 Closes.

5 The fire dies on the ashes created by its own earlier (youthful) burning.

74: 1 Dreaded.
2 This poem.
3 Always.
4 Its.

75: 1 As food is to existence (essential).
2 The peace to be found in loving you.
3 (i) counting on, depending on, (ii) counting as a miser counts money.
4 Pleased better.
5 All (food taken) away.

76: 1 New fashions (in writing poetry).
2 Strange new poetic inventions.
3 Clothing.
4 Constantly.

77: 1 Mirror.
2 Pages (of a book or journal).
3 The creations written on the blank pages.
4 Duties.

78: 1 Several of the next sonnets compare the writer's verse with another writer (the rival poet), often unfavourably.
2 Every other writer has my inspiration.
3 Circulate.
4 Excellence
5 My own verses.

79: 1 Melodious verses.
2 Give way to another writer.
3 The youth as an attractive subject.

80: 1 The rival poet.
2 Small boat.
3 Ocean.
4 Bottomless.
5 Solid construction.

81: 1 Either.
2 (i) this poem, (ii) the world.
3 Power.

82: 1 The following two sonnets can be read together, with the image of painting continued between them.
2 Dishonour.
3 Devoted words (punning on a poet's dedication of his work to a patron).
4 Exceeding the limits of my ability to praise.
5 Modern days, improving on earlier times.
6 Expressed.
7 Description, punning on the use of makeup.

83: 1 Your beauty.
2 Worthless offer (the metaphor is of money).
3 Alive.
4 My silence does not damage your beauty, whereas others, in trying to bring it to life, fail, and bury it.

84: 1 The most excessive praise can say no more.
2 In you the abundance is contained (walled in).
3 Poverty.
4 Such an equivalent shall make his wit famous.
5 Doting on.

85: 1 Preserve your qualities.
2 Polished.
3 Uneducated.
4 The highest praise.
5 Thought's (*his* here means *its*).

86: 1 The rival poet's
2 As in a pirate's prize, taking a ship captive.
3 Place in a coffin.
4 The evil spirits that are assisting the rival poet.
5 Deceives him with ideas.
6 When your face provided the inspiration for his lines.

87: 1 Value. The sustained metaphor in this sonnet is of legal contracts concerning property.
2 Contract, privilege.
3 Ended, terminated.
4 Lacking.

<table>
<tr><td></td><td>5</td><td>Right (of possession).</td></tr>
<tr><td></td><td>6</td><td>Misunderstanding.</td></tr>
<tr><td>88:</td><td>1</td><td>Treat me lightly.</td></tr>
<tr><td></td><td>2</td><td>Taking your side.</td></tr>
<tr><td></td><td>3</td><td>Dishonoured.</td></tr>
<tr><td>89:</td><td>1</td><td>The next group of sonnets contains some pairs that are ideally read together, as creating a kind of dialogue.</td></tr>
<tr><td></td><td>2</td><td>Limp.</td></tr>
<tr><td></td><td>3</td><td>To rationalize a change you desire.</td></tr>
<tr><td></td><td>4</td><td>I will stifle our friendship and pretend not to know you.</td></tr>
<tr><td></td><td>5</td><td>Accidentally.</td></tr>
<tr><td>90:</td><td>1</td><td>Wait to add to my loss.</td></tr>
<tr><td></td><td>2</td><td>Come after I have recovered from sorrow.</td></tr>
<tr><td></td><td>3</td><td>To protract.</td></tr>
<tr><td>91:</td><td>1</td><td>Though they are ugly new fashions.</td></tr>
<tr><td>92:</td><td>1</td><td>This sonnet should be read together with number 93.</td></tr>
<tr><td></td><td>2</td><td>The loss of friendship, seemingly a lesser problem.</td></tr>
<tr><td></td><td>3</td><td>Whims.</td></tr>
<tr><td></td><td>4</td><td>Since my life depends (will end) when you revolt (deny my love).</td></tr>
<tr><td>93:</td><td>1</td><td>Believing.</td></tr>
<tr><td></td><td>2</td><td>The consistent contrast between the eye, which sees only the surface, and the heart, which holds the true feeling.</td></tr>
<tr><td>94:</td><td>1</td><td>This and the following sonnet can be read as an interconnected pair.</td></tr>
<tr><td></td><td>2</td><td>Seem to do, are capable of doing.</td></tr>
<tr><td></td><td>3</td><td>Preserve.</td></tr>
<tr><td></td><td>4</td><td>Servants.</td></tr>
<tr><td>95:</td><td>1</td><td>Love affairs.</td></tr>
<tr><td></td><td>2</td><td>Unlimited (also with the sense of morally loose).</td></tr>
<tr><td>96:</td><td>1</td><td>Playfulness, lechery.</td></tr>
<tr><td></td><td>2</td><td>Courtly amorousness.</td></tr>
<tr><td></td><td>3</td><td>Loved by people of high and low rank.</td></tr>
<tr><td></td><td>4</td><td>Convert.</td></tr>
<tr><td></td><td>5</td><td>Reputation. The same final couplet is used in sonnet 36.</td></tr>
<tr><td>97:</td><td>1</td><td>i.e. the summer.</td></tr>
<tr><td></td><td>2</td><td>Pregnant.</td></tr>
<tr><td></td><td>3</td><td>Carrying the fruit (crops) conceived by the spring (*prime*).</td></tr>
<tr><td></td><td>4</td><td>Offspring.</td></tr>
<tr><td></td><td>5</td><td>Such a melancholy mood.</td></tr>
<tr><td>98:</td><td>1</td><td>Gorgeously multicoloured.</td></tr>
<tr><td></td><td>2</td><td>Associated with melancholy; Saturn was also the god of agriculture and fertility, both connected with the spring.</td></tr>
<tr><td></td><td>3</td><td>Songs.</td></tr>
<tr><td></td><td>4</td><td>Neither.</td></tr>
<tr><td></td><td>5</td><td>Images.</td></tr>
<tr><td></td><td>6</td><td>Portrait (literal, or in words).</td></tr>
<tr><td>99:</td><td>1</td><td>This irregular sonnet has fifteen lines.</td></tr>
<tr><td></td><td>2</td><td>Early-flowering, with a sense of presumptuousness.</td></tr>
<tr><td></td><td>3</td><td>Excessively.</td></tr>
<tr><td></td><td>4</td><td>Neither.</td></tr>
<tr><td></td><td>5</td><td>Budworm.</td></tr>
<tr><td></td><td>6</td><td>This extra line adds a fifth to the normal quatrain; arguably it emphasizes the strong feeling of revenge the line suggests.</td></tr>
<tr><td>100:</td><td>1</td><td>Inspiration.</td></tr>
<tr><td></td><td>2</td><td>Abasing.</td></tr>
<tr><td></td><td>3</td><td>Elegant verses.</td></tr>
<tr><td></td><td>4</td><td>Songs.</td></tr>
<tr><td></td><td>5</td><td>Subject matter.</td></tr>
<tr><td></td><td>6</td><td>Restless.</td></tr>
<tr><td></td><td>7</td><td>(His Muse should) mock the process of decay.</td></tr>
<tr><td>101:</td><td>1</td><td>Truth made integral with beauty.</td></tr>
<tr><td></td><td>2</td><td>Justification.</td></tr>
<tr><td></td><td>3</td><td>Express.</td></tr>
<tr><td></td><td>4</td><td>To make him seem to the future as he is now.</td></tr>
</table>

<table>
<tr><td>102:</td><td>1</td><td>Cheapened, as if for sale.</td></tr>
<tr><td></td><td>2</td><td>Value.</td></tr>
<tr><td></td><td>3</td><td>Was used to.</td></tr>
<tr><td></td><td>4</td><td>Songs.</td></tr>
<tr><td></td><td>5</td><td>The nightingale.</td></tr>
<tr><td></td><td>6</td><td>The beginning.</td></tr>
<tr><td></td><td>7</td><td>Weighs down; with a pun on *burden* meaning the chorus of a song.</td></tr>
<tr><td>103:</td><td>1</td><td>Poor verse.</td></tr>
<tr><td></td><td>2</td><td>The subject itself, unadorned.</td></tr>
<tr><td></td><td>3</td><td>Mirror.</td></tr>
<tr><td></td><td>4</td><td>Purpose.</td></tr>
<tr><td>104:</td><td>1</td><td>This sonnet gives the clearest indication of the length of time over which the Sonnets were written.</td></tr>
<tr><td></td><td>2</td><td>The dial of the clock moves, though its movement is imperceptible.</td></tr>
<tr><td></td><td>3</td><td>Is unchanged.</td></tr>
<tr><td>105:</td><td>1</td><td>Appear.</td></tr>
<tr><td></td><td>2</td><td>Focused on one person and subject; the argument is that such constancy cannot be considered wrong.</td></tr>
<tr><td></td><td>3</td><td>Variation (in words only).</td></tr>
<tr><td></td><td>4</td><td>The writer is flirting with idolatry as he denies it, since he is echoing, almost parodying, the doctrine of the Trinity.</td></tr>
<tr><td>106:</td><td>1</td><td>Past, useless.</td></tr>
<tr><td></td><td>2</td><td>People.</td></tr>
<tr><td></td><td>3</td><td>Formal, heraldic description.</td></tr>
<tr><td></td><td>4</td><td>Old-fashioned.</td></tr>
<tr><td></td><td>5</td><td>Prophetic.</td></tr>
<tr><td>107:</td><td>1</td><td>The spirit of humankind, imagining the future.</td></tr>
<tr><td></td><td>2</td><td>Ending date.</td></tr>
<tr><td></td><td>3</td><td>Imagined that there was to be a specific ending (use-by date).</td></tr>
<tr><td></td><td>4</td><td>This line is usually read as a reference to Queen Elizabeth, and may recall her death in 1603.</td></tr>
<tr><td></td><td>5</td><td>Solemn prophets revise their own predictions.</td></tr>
<tr><td></td><td>6</td><td>Peace is assured (possibly referring to the optimism at the accession of James of Scotland to the English throne).</td></tr>
<tr><td></td><td>7</td><td>Peaceful, or prosperous.</td></tr>
<tr><td></td><td>8</td><td>Yields.</td></tr>
<tr><td></td><td>9</td><td>Consumed, destroyed.</td></tr>
<tr><td>108:</td><td>1</td><td>Record in handwriting.</td></tr>
<tr><td></td><td>2</td><td>Illustrated.</td></tr>
<tr><td></td><td>3</td><td>Assuming nothing to be hackneyed or a cliché.</td></tr>
<tr><td></td><td>4</td><td>Servant.</td></tr>
<tr><td></td><td>5</td><td>Thoughts.</td></tr>
<tr><td>109:</td><td>1</td><td>In the next four sonnets, the writer attempts to atone for a seeming failure in friendship, possibly a scandal (see 112), or simply the writer's trade as actor and playwright.</td></tr>
<tr><td></td><td>2</td><td>Ardency of love to abate.</td></tr>
<tr><td></td><td>3</td><td>Strayed.</td></tr>
<tr><td></td><td>4</td><td>Exactly on time.</td></tr>
<tr><td></td><td>5</td><td>Fault (leaving the loved one).</td></tr>
<tr><td></td><td>6</td><td>Passions.</td></tr>
<tr><td>110:</td><td>1</td><td>In this sonnet, Shakespeare seems to be criticizing himself as a mere actor, one who dons the *motley* clothing of the Fool (on stage).</td></tr>
<tr><td></td><td>2</td><td>Jester.</td></tr>
<tr><td></td><td>3</td><td>Damaged.</td></tr>
<tr><td></td><td>4</td><td>New passions.</td></tr>
<tr><td></td><td>5</td><td>Flinchings or swervings, possibly deceits.</td></tr>
<tr><td></td><td>6</td><td>Less successful attempts.</td></tr>
<tr><td>111:</td><td>1</td><td>Who.</td></tr>
<tr><td></td><td>2</td><td>Fortune has dictated that the writer must make a living in the public realm (as actor and playwright), which makes him behave like a commoner.</td></tr>
<tr><td></td><td>3</td><td>Disgrace (criminals were branded).</td></tr>
<tr><td></td><td>4</td><td>The dyer's hand becomes permanently stained.</td></tr>
<tr><td></td><td>5</td><td>Vinegar.</td></tr>
<tr><td></td><td>6</td><td>Vinegar was used as a supposed protection against the plague.</td></tr>
</table>

112: 1 Wrinkle.
2 Possibly another reference to his craft as actor.
3 Cover (with new growth).
4 No one else matters.
5 Hardened.
6 The hearing – adders (snakes) were supposed to be deaf.
113: 1 The part of me that directs my actions.
2 It seems to see, but is not functioning.
3 Perceive.
4 Its living surroundings.
5 The eye.
6 My mind, being true to you, makes my perception false.
114: 1 Either (connected to the same phrase two lines later).
2 Capacity to convert the ugly to beauty, as the alchemists changed base metal to gold.
3 Formless.
4 Angels.
5 His "eyebeams".
6 Taste
115: 1 Time, which both counts and provides an ultimate reckoning, and its countless unforeseen circumstances.
2 Darken, as with age, or exposure to the sun.
3 Time causes even the strong-minded to change according to altered circumstances.
4 Certain in the face of the uncertain future.
5 As figured in Cupid.
116: 1 Allow problems; the word echoes the marriage service in the Book of Common Prayer.
2 When it finds change in the object of love.
3 The *remover* here is possibly disease or misfortune.
4 Ship.
5 The elevation of the (North) star is known, but not its value.
6 The sickle, used for reaping, is a symbol of the passage of time.
117: 1 Neglected.
2 Deservings.
3 Familiar.
4 Record.
5 Add suspicion to proof.
6 Aim. The metaphor is from archery, as in the following line.
7 As in a legal appeal of a verdict.
118: 1 Just as.
2 Sharp-flavoured spices.
3 Take medicines to purge (by induced vomiting or diarrhoea). The medical metaphor is extended over the next lines.
4 Appropriateness.
5 Strategy.
6 Overfed with good (health).
7 Medicines.
119: 1 Tempting. The Sirens sang songs so beautiful that they bewitched sailors such that they were wrecked on the neighbouring rocks; there may be a suggestion of an affair.
2 Apparatus used for distillation; the beauty of the perfume distilled is contrasted with the ugliness of the still.
3 Continually.
4 Have bulged (in the fever).
120: 1 Makes me feel better.
2 I must feel the weight of the wrong I have committed.
3 Have not taken the time.
4 Consider.
5 Reminded.
6 Offered.
7 Medicinal ointment.
8 The earlier indiscretion.
121: 1 One might as well behave badly, and have the

fun of doing so, if others are going to assume that you have been indiscreet.
2 The others' eyes judge by their own falseness.
3 Spontaneous moods, or passions.
4 Aim.
5 Biased.
6 Decaying, foul.
122: 1 Book of memorandums, journal.
2 Written.
3 The pages of the book (less important than the actual memories).
4 Both heart and brain.
5 The book itself.
6 The metaphor is of sticks marked to keep score of money owing.
7 Imply.
123: 1 These newer pyramids may refer to structures built in London to welcome James I in 1603.
2 Life is short.
3 Time.
4 Records.
124: 1 In this case, the emotion of love, not the person the poem is directed to.
2 Circumstances.
3 It might be considered the illegitimate result of chance.
4 Comfortable luxury.
5 The discontent of those oppressed.
6 Which the current times see as fashionable.
7 Pragmatic self-interest (which does not take the long view).
8 Prudent.
9 Neither.
10 Those who live only for the present.
125: 1 Did it matter.
2 A decorative shade carried over a dignitary.
3 Acknowledging external honour.
4 Plans.
5 External forms and currying favour.
6 Attention.
7 Ignoring simple tastes in favour of excessive sweetness.
8 Pitiful spendthrifts, bankrupted in their excessive admiration (of those they seek to impress).
9 Devoted.
10 Offering (the term is used in a religious context).
11 Is not adulterated.
12 Rendering, exchange.
13 Bribed witness (presumably the person who accused the Poet of flattery).
126: 1 This "sonnet" consists of six couplets, and concludes the first section, of poems presumably addressed to the youth.
2 Hourglass.
3 Grown (in beauty) by getting older.
4 Decay.
5 Continually.
6 Favourite.
7 Forever.
8 The traditional reckoning at death.
9 Final settlement.
10 Give thee up.
127: 1 This is the first of the poems written to the dark woman.
2 Olden days (of traditional, Petrarchan love poetry).
3 Proclaimed heir to the name of beauty.
4 Previous (fair/blonde) beauty.
5 Illegitimate because acquired through artificial means (see the following lines).
6 The use of artificial makeup.
7 No place of refuge.
8 Bringing naturally created beauty into disrespect by their artificial good looks.

9 Her eyes.

10 Gracing.

128: 1 In this sonnet, the dark woman is playing on a virginal or early harpsichord.

2 His mistress.

3 The keyboard.

4 The harmony of the strings.

5 Technically, the device that plucks the string when the key is depressed; here more likely a reference to the keys themselves (see the pun in the penultimate line).

6 The keys (chips of wood).

7 Punningly for cheeky knaves.

129: 1 This deeply troubling sonnet recalls the difficult sexual world of *Troilus and Cressida* and *Measure for Measure* (see pp. 206 and 210 below); see also the Introduction to this section, p.30.

2 Vital spirits; the orgasm was seen as spending vital energy.

3 With a pun on *waist*.

130: 1 In this sonnet, the Poet mocks the tradition of Petrarchan verse with its ideal of blonde beauty.

2 Beige.

3 (Golden) wires.

4 Variegated.

5 Walk.

131: 1 Just as you are: dark.

2 Only by.

3 One after another.

132: 1 To torment.

2 Pity.

3 Suits.

4 Be appropriate for.

5 Dress.

133: 1 The next two sonnets suggest that the dark woman has had an affair with a friend, possibly the youth. See also sonnet 144.

2 Curse.

3 Totally enslaved.

4 His friend.

5 Literally, bought up wholesale; possibly with overtones of *gross*, overfed.

6 Suffered.

7 Cell.

8 Imprisoned.

134: 1 (i) wishes, (ii) sexual appetite.

2 The youth.

3 As in providing a bond for bail.

4 To gain interest.

135: 1 The next two sonnets make much of punning on Shakespeare's name, Will, associating it with the term *will* as applied to sexual desire, passion, and free will.

2 (By adding myself.)

3 As the modern slang term *willy* suggests, there is a sexual pun.

4 (i) let no unkind act disappoint those who seek your favours, (ii) let no unkind "no" disappoint them.

136: 1 Rebuke.

2 That my comments are so accurate (also physically near).

3 The soul, unreceptive to the senses.

4 Fill the treasury (with sexual suggestion).

5 Great capacity (suggesting that she has many like him).

6 A single one is trivial; the Elizabethan saying was "one is no number".

7 Consider me to be nothing.

137: 1 Cupid, traditionally portrayed as blind.

2 Biased.

3 The metaphor is of a ship in a busy harbour; the suggestion is that the mistress is profligate.

4 Separate, individual.

138: 1 This subtle and ironic poem treats the mutual

falsehoods of the writer and the dark woman with a light touch.

2 In vain; also self-deceivingly.

3 Foolishly I believe.

4 Why.

5 Counted up, totalled.

6 (i) tell lies, (ii) sleep with.

139: 1 Do not ask me to rationalize your falseness. Compare the writer's ready excuses for the youth's behaviour.

2 Be direct, not artful.

3 So he does rationalize her behaviour after all.

4 At others.

140: 1 (i) unpitied, (ii) pity-desiring.

2 To tell me that you love me, even if you do not.

3 Irritable.

4 Twisting everything to the worst meaning possible.

5 Again the image of the roving eye.

141: 1 Love foolishly.

2 Nor is my sense of touch attracted to you.

3 The five *wits* were these: common sense, imagination, fantasy, judgement, and memory.

4 (The heart) leaves him with no control, and thus only a shell of a person.

142: 1 Her strength is to hate him – a virtue since he is sinning in loving her.

2 Lips, but also the red seal that makes a legal document (*bond*) valid.

3 Committed adultery with others (stealing the husbands' love – and semen – from their wives).

4 Beg of.

5 Make you deserving.

6 The pity she is withholding.

143: 1 One of the few comic touches in the sequence, this sonnet pictures the Poet as a crying child running after its mother.

2 Hens or geese.

3 Soothe.

144: 1 This deeply bitter sonnet is usually taken as confirmation of an affair between the dark woman and the youth.

2 One comforting (the youth), one creating despair (the dark woman).

3 Tempt. The writer imagines the two loves like one good and one evil angel, each trying to win him over.

4 Has fallen (as the rebellious angels fell from heaven).

5 Away from.

6 With sexual suggestion of intercourse.

7 The implication may be that the dark woman will pass on a sexually transmitted disease.

145: 1 Written in shorter, octosyllabic lines, this sonnet may be from an earlier period in Shakespeare's life. There is a probable pun on Hathaway in the penultimate line: "'I hate' from '*hate' away* she threw."

2 Passing a mild sentence.

146: 1 Another unique sonnet, in its focus on spiritual questions.

2 Body.

3 These words are one of a number of conjectured emendations; the original repeats the words "my sinful earth" from the previous line.

4 Held captive by sin that surrounds it.

5 While there is famine (*dearth*) within, he dresses his body in fine clothes.

6 His short-lived, physical body.

7 The body's.

8 Trade worthless hours spent on pleasure (*dross*) for time (*terms*) in heaven.

147: 1 Finicky.

2 Crazed, irrational.

3 Prove by experience.

4 Forbid.

148: 1 Accurate connection with.
      2 Judges.
      3 Staying awake.
149: 1 Take your side against myself.
      2 Frownest.
      3 Immediate complaint.
      4 Value.
150: 1 Shortcomings.
      2 Fair beauty (since she is dark, and associated with night).
      3 Making attractive.
      4 Assurance.
      5 Your worst exceeds all that is best.
151: 1 Cupid is figured as a child.
      2 Guilty conscience; knowledge of sexuality and the attendant sin.
      3 Soul.
      4 As in an erection (the pun continues in the following lines).
      5 Swollen with.
152: 1 Faithless.
153: 1 The final two sonnets, to Cupid, seem to be from an earlier period in Shakespeare's career.
      2 A torch (we still use the term); there is also a sexual suggestion in the image.
      3 Goddess of the moon and chastity.
      4 In that area.
      5 Heated (literally *boiling*).
      6 Highly effective.
      7 To test the re-lit torch.
      8 Hurried.
      9 Sick; baths were used as a cure for venereal disease, often described as fiery.
154: 1 Vowed to chastity.
      2 Organizer, Cupid.

VENUS AND ADONIS

1 From *The First Part of the Return from Parnassus*, cited by Schoenberg, p.131.
2 Hurries.
3 Begins.
4 Making all nymphs seem ugly by comparison.
5 Says.
6 Reward.
7 Her white arms (a *pale* is a fence).
8 Grass in a valley; *brakes* are thickets.
9 A dumb show: a mime; the theatrical analogy continues in the next line with the *chorus*, traditionally commenting on the main action.
10 Surrounds, clasps.
11 To keep awake.
12 All remains in her imagination.
13 Tantalus was surrounded in Hades by food and drink that he could not reach, in punishment for serving his son as a sacrifice to the gods.
14 In Greek mythology, the dwelling of the virtuous after death.
15 Mouth.
16 Tusks.
17 Hackneyed. Venus has just ended a passage pleading on behalf of love.
18 Too young.
19 In seriousness.
20 Regret.
21 Clearing.
22 Separate.
23 The lids of treasure chests.
24 Past the stage of being full-blown; an intensified use of the word.
25 Strewn over.
26 Venus's home in Cyprus.
27 To hide herself behind the walls of her palace.

A MIDSUMMER NIGHT'S DREAM

1 Probably.
2 Flood.

3 Inherited social rank.
4 Badly matched.
5 Darkened (as with coal).
6 In a sudden impulse.

LOVE'S LABOUR'S LOST

1 A parish constable.
2 A school-teacher.
3 Muffled.
4 Completely blind.
5 Sir.
6 Lovers were traditionally figured with their arms folded across the breast.
7 The placket is a slit in a petticoat; the codpiece the rather more visible equivalent of the trouser fly.
8 Police for the Ecclesiastical Court, who had the power to arrest those suspected of sexual offences.
9 An officer in his army.
10 A mythological monster with a hundred eyes.
11 A barbarian who worships the sun.
12 A resolute eye. The eagle was fabled to be able to look directly at the sun without harm.
13 Those chosen as the best.
14 Lacks.
15 Berowne at first thinks to use elaborate rhetorical devices, then decides that they are unnecessary. Compare with Sonnet 21.
16 A hundred (five times twenty).
17 A Bible to swear on.
18 The King is perhaps referring back to his earlier assertion that his love, the Princess, is like the moon, while Rosaline is merely an attendant star.
19 Women using makeup and wigs.
20 Coal-miners.
21 Subtle arguments.
22 Medicine.
23 Passionate verses.
24 Confined.
25 Hearing becomes as acute as the ear of a thief hearing a sound.
26 By horns, Berowne means the snail's eye-stalks; cockled, having a shell.
27 God of wine and legendary gourmet.
28 One of Hercules' labours was to pluck the golden apples from the garden of the Hesperides.
29 The Sphinx that guarded the entrance to the city of Thebes posed a riddle to all who tried to pass: "What animal is that which in the morning goes on four feet, at noon on two, and in the evening upon three?" Hercules correctly answered "man", who crawls when young, walks when mature, and needs a cane when old.
30 Apollo, god of the sun, poetry and music.
31 Prometheus stole fire from the gods to give it to humans.
32 In our discussions considered them.
33 As padding and unnecessary material (the metaphor is taken from clothing: bombast originally meant shredded material used for creating the characteristic bulges in Renaissance costume.
34 Scornful jokes.
35 All people, regardless of rank.
36 A bitter herb.

ROMEO AND JULIET

1 Blind – the traditional image of Cupid.
2 Very much the adolescent male, Romeo is as much interested in food as love.
3 Gall is proverbially bitter.
4 Dance.
5 Break any earlier oath to the contrary.
6 Juliet's hand.
7 Punningly; a palmer was a pilgrim who had been to Jerusalem and brought back a palm leaf.
8 The images of saints remain motionless, though they may grant the wishes of those who pray to them.

9   A fruit that was eaten when beginning to decay; its appearance was jokingly likened to female sexual organs.
10 A slang name for the medlar.
11 An elongated pear; used here with sexual suggestiveness.
12 Folding bed.
13 The ground.
14 A vestal virgin, follower of Diana, goddess of the moon and chastity.
15 The uniform of Diana's virginal followers.
16 The heavenly crystal spheres that were thought to sustain the stars and planets as they orbited the Earth.
17 Why are you called Romeo (a Montague)?
18 Take off (as with clothes).
19 Fly above.
20 Delayed.
21 Conventional courtly behaviour.
22 Ruler of the gods.
23 Infatuated.
24 My behaviour indecorous.
25 Standoffish.
26 Direction.
27 A male hawk, trained for hunting.
28 A spoiled child's.
29 Fetters, chains.
30 God of the sun, whose chariot of fire was drawn by horses across the sky.
31 Son of Phoebus (Helios), who drove the horses wildly across the sky; an example of excessive ambition and haste that Juliet ironically invokes.
32 Close.
33 Teach.
34 Beating, or flapping. Juliet is using imagery from hawking; the hawk was tamed by being hooded.
35 Joyful.
36 Notes out of tune.
37 Improvisational melody.
38 Flag. Romeo does not realize that this is a sign of Juliet's recovery.
39 Always.
40 Misfortune, through the influence of the stars.
41 The poison, acting as a guide to the afterlife.
42 Ship.
43 The equivalent of the police.
44 (i) untimely, (ii) endless.

THE MERCHANT OF VENICE
1   See the selection from Shakespeare's play on this legend below.
2   Shakespeare parodies the tragic story of Pyramus and Thisbe in the play-within-the-play of *A Midsummer Night's Dream*.
3   Dido, Queen of Carthage, was deserted by Aeneas and committed suicide.
4   A symbol of unrequited love. Desdemona sings the beautiful "willow" song before her death in Othello; see pp.223–5.
5   Medea helped Jason win the golden fleece, then restored youth to his father Aeson.
6   The location of this scene, Portia's estate.
7   Are appropriate for.
8   Plates of metal.
9   Our physical body.
10 Goddess of the moon.
11 Another term for herd.
12 A dark place between the Earth and Hades.

TWELFTH NIGHT
1   Overdosing.
2   Melodic phrase.
3   Although love can seem as boundless as the sea, all feelings, no matter how high they soar, will in due course lose value.
4   The imagination; possibly here meaning love.
5   Fantastic, unreal.

AS YOU LIKE IT
1   Celia.
2   Rabbit.
3   Littered, or born.
4   One who lives in the city.
5   Medicine.
6   Seller of love.
7   Fever.
8   Flimsy cage.
9   Rosalind cheekily suggests that Orlando is too young to have a beard.
10 All these marks suggest someone careless about their appearance.
11 Excessively neat.
12 Clothes.
13 In truth.
14 The mentally ill were routinely controlled by prison and punishment.
15 Changeable, like the moon.
16 She drove him from love-madness to real madness.
17 Thought to be the seat of the passions.
18 Cottage.
19 True. (She is pretending to be the youth, pretending to be Rosalind.)
20 Perplexed.
21 When they have lost their inspiration for a moment.
22 I would think my chastity fouler than my wit.
23 Rosalind puns on the two meanings of suit: a request (from Orlando) and a suit of clothes.
24 Die by proxy.
25 In pre-Darwinian times, the world was calculated to have been created in 4000 BCE.
26 That is to say (Latin).
27 The legend of Hero and Leander – according to which Leander was drowned swimming across the Strait of the Dardanelles (the Hellespont) to see his loved one.
28 Licence.
29 Fascinated by novelty.
30 Rosalind is apparently thinking of an ornamental fountain, featuring the goddess Diana.

MUCH ADO ABOUT NOTHING
1   Solemnly, seriously.
2   Witty comments.
3   Spoken and written words.
4   The pursuit of his desire.
5   Blackbird.
6   Appetite.
7   You have stopped me just in time.
8   Proved.
9   Delude her.
10 Claudio is a Count.
11 A sweetmeat.
12 Claudio's – in order to challenge him to a duel herself.
13 Men are all talk, no action.
14 Committed to challenging him to a duel.
15 Pay dearly for his actions.
16 Go-betweens in a liaison; pimps.
17 Former wooers (those associated with carpeted chambers).
18 Publicize.

RICHARD III
1   Shakespeare's portrayal of Richard, deeply influenced by Tudor propaganda, has been challenged. See, for further information, the website of the Richard III Society, <http://www.richardiii.net/begin.htm>.
2   Guards carrying halberds, or long pole-axes.
3   The death of Henry VI, and the demise of the House of Lancaster as a result.
4   Wounds.
5   Fortune.
6   Unnatural.
7   A monastery near London.
8   Trample.

9 Begone. "Avaunt" was often used to frighten off an evil spirit.
10 Only.
11 It was a common belief that a person's wounds would bleed afresh in the presence of the person who murdered them.
12 Draws forth.
13 Alive.
14 Feels.
15 Bestow, permit.
16 Detailed explanation.
17 Confused.
18 The crest of Richard's family featured a boar, here exaggerated to become a spiny hedgehog.
19 Both the houses of York and Lancaster were Plantagenets. The death of Richard III ended the dynasty, as Henry VII began the reign of the Tudors.
20 Mythical beasts who killed simply by looking.
21 Consent.
22 I take the ring, but make no promises.
23 Richard uses the courtly term for one who is committed to love.
24 A small copper coin of proverbially little value.

TROILUS AND CRESSIDA
1 Mirror.
2 No woman has ever found consummated love as intense as love stimulated by frustrated desire.
3 Men will command women they have conquered, but will beg for favours from those they have yet to win.
4 Mouth-watering.
5 Frightened by a spirit.
6 Used here as a term of endearment.
7 Serfs, servants.
8 Kept awake. Pandarus is thinking of the process of taming hawks.
9 The shafts of a cart.
10 Pandarus uses terms from the game of lawn bowls, where the target ball is the "mistress".
11 Lands granted in perpetuity were fee-farm; thus the kiss is a long one.
12 Again from hawking: Pandarus puts his money on the falcon (the female) to capture more ducks than the tercel (the male).
13 As in billing and cooing.
14 A legal formula for contracts.
15 Breaking-off.
16 The dreg is the unpalatable sediment at the bottom of a liquid.
17 An angelic child, often portrayed in Renaissance artworks.
18 Challenges.

MEASURE FOR MEASURE
1 The violet blooms in the strength (virtue) of the sun, while the same sun causes the carrion to rot.
2 Sensuality.
3 Immodesty.
4 In his pride, Angelo sees himself as a saint.

OTHELLO
1 Continually.
2 Exciting.
3 A break-though in fortifications.
4 Flexible, spare time.
5 Describe in detail.
6 With full attention.
7 Brabantio earlier accused Othello of using spells to enchant Desdemona.
8 Make the best of a bad deal.
9 Teach.
10 One to whom I owe my dutiful obedience.
11 Official authorization.
12 Desdemona takes some pride in her unconventional behaviour.
13 Desdemona values Othello's mind over his appearance.
14 Qualities.
15 Moths were the example of wasteful consumers.
16 Marital rites, with a pun on "rights".
17 Sexual desire. Othello claims to be too old for such trifles.
18 Neglect.
19 Blind, as hawks were blinded in training, by sewing up their eyes.
20 His eyes.
21 Pleasures.
22 Undignified.
23 Raise an army against my reputation.
24 The "fig" was the equivalent of giving the finger to someone.
25 A medicinal herb.
26 The power to correct something.
27 Weigh against.
28 Unrestrained (as a horse is restrained by the bit).
29 Branch.
30 Ending.
31 Fruit of the carob (often used as a substitute for chocolate), not the insect.
32 A bitter fruit used as a purgative.
33 Iago belittles the sacred bond of marriage.
34 Ship.
35 Mount Olympus was the supposed seat of the gods.
36 A husband whose wife has been unfaithful.
37 Without end.
38 Decided
39 Inflated and exaggerated (flyblown).
40 The patterns of behaviour in our country.
41 Acknowledged.
42 Thoughts.
43 The passions.
44 Neither opium nor mandrake (a poisonous herb with hallucinogenic and soporific qualities).
45 The willow was traditionally associated with disappointed love.
46 A ring made with interlocking halves.
47 Fine material.
48 Gift.
49 God's pity.
50 The metaphor is from gambling; enough to stock the whole of the world they are gambling for.
51 Pour our sexual treasure – she implies semen – into the laps of other women.
52 Or spitefully reduce what we have been accustomed to have.
53 Feelings of bitterness.
54 Appetites.
55 Sexual pleasure.
56 Feeling, passion.
57 Marble.
58 He is referring to a candle.
59 In separate myths, Prometheus was both the creator of humankind, and the one who stole fire from the gods for them.
60 Manipulated.
61 In the other early text of the play, the word here is "Judean", making a reference to Judas rather than to the inhabitants of the new colonies, of whom captives were recently brought back to England.
62 He is referring to myrrh.

ANTONY AND CLEOPATRA
1 God of war; plated: in armour.
2 On the dark-complexioned face of Cleopatra.
3 Abandons all moderation.
4 As one member of the governing triumvirate, Antony commands one third of the world.
5 A boundary or limit.
6 Do not admit that I sent you.
7 Polished.
8 The rear deck, raised.

9 Masochistically, the water followed the oars that beat it.
10 Her sunshade, made of diaphanous material with gold thread interwoven.
11 She was more a work of art than an artwork where the artist seems to outshine nature.
12 The act of cooling by fanning seemed paradoxically to heat her cheeks.
13 Sea nymphs.
14 Even their bowing was decorative.
15 Skilfully.
16 Even the air would have gone to gaze on Cleopatra, if it would not have created a vacuum.
17 The price of the meal.
18 Cleopatra had earlier had Julius Caesar as a lover, by whom she bore a son, Caesarion.
19 Enobarbus again stresses Cleopatra's paradoxical nature.
20 Become appropriate.
21 Sexually active.
22 Fishing-rod.
23 Clothes.
24 The sun, like all the heavenly bodies were thought to be held in place by crystalline spheres.
25 In the dark.
26 Plead with.
27 She dares not descend for fear of capture.
28 Proud.
29 Adorned (Caesar would lead her in triumph in Rome).
30 Quiet manners.
31 Looking demurely.
32 Sadness.
33 Juno was Jove's wife; Mercury was the winged messenger of the gods, the only god able to travel between the realm of the living and the dead.
34 Come alive.
35 Housewife (demeaningly); hussy.
36 Wilt thou.
37 Flag, standard.
38 Differences in rank and gender.
39 Foolish.
40 Commit suicide.
41 Body.
42 Quickly.
43 The good luck that the gods give men, so that they can punish them afterwards.
44 Antony is married to Octavia, but Cleopatra believes that the nobility of her death will earn her the right to call him her husband. Caesar does in fact bury her by his side.
45 Earth and water, the baser of the four elements.
46 The poison of the asp.
47 If you die so gently.
48 Antony in all his finery; Cleopatra is jealous lest Iras see him and kiss him before her in the afterlife.
49 Intricate.
50 Lacking in political knowhow.
51 She refers to the asp.
52 Eyelids.
53 God of the sun.

THE WINTER'S TALE

1 One good deed unrecognized means that many more will never happen because of the lack of praise.
2 One eighth of a mile.
3 Run over, as in a race. Leontes picks up on the metaphor of (sexual) heat later.
4 Call.
5 Sexual intercourse was thought to involve the mixing of blood from both partners.
6 Palpitations of the heart.
7 An innocent appearance.
8 A generous heart. But remember that the Hermione Leontes sees is pregnant.
9 Be admired.

10 The bugle call that signalled that a deer had been brought down in the hunt.
11 Leontes is thinking, obsessively, of the supposed horns sported by a cuckold – a man whose wife has been unfaithful.
12 Spectacles (Camillo is usually acted by an older man).
13 Obsessively, Leontes is thinking of the protective cover of thin, transparent horn placed over often-read pages to protect them.
14 Such an obvious sight.
15 Not eyes, ears or thought.
16 A loose woman (so called from the child's toy).
17 Common countrywoman.
18 Has sex before her engagement.
19 Beshrew, curse.
20 Playing with feet under the table.
21 Leontes' paranoia becomes clear as he states as fact what he believes they are thinking.
22 Cataract formations in the eye.
23 Of course, Bohemia, forming part of the modern Czech Republic, has no sea coast; but this is a winter's tale, where anything is possible.
24 According to Ovid, Proserpina was gathering flowers when she was abducted by Pluto (a.k.a. Dis) and taken into the underworld.
25 An alternative name for Venus, goddess of love.
26 The god of the sun.
27 Perdita likens the pale colour of the primrose to young girls, prone to anaemia.
28 An imported flower grown in English gardens.
29 Alive.
30 Festivities at Whitsun (seven weeks after Easter), often including folk dances.
31 Perform.
32 So special in each detail.
33 Each act seems superior to the ones that preceded it.
34 Florizel's assumed name.
35 Too exaggerated.
36 Virtuous.
37 That you were trying to seduce me.
38 Turtledoves; traditionally mating for life.
39 Grass.
40 That makes her blush.
41 As accurately imitated.
42 As if.
43 Piece of sculpture.
44 The statue has magically conjured his memories of Hermione to return.
45 Vital spirits, as Perdita stands awestruck.
46 As if.
47 Heartwarming.
48 Strike up the music.
49 From Death.
50 There may be a hidden stage direction here as Leontes draws back.
51 If she is truly alive.
52 Paulina seems to be thinking of the process of anointing with holy oils.
53 At this crucial moment.
54 Shakespeare never resolves this seeming contradiction; either Hermione has been miraculously brought back to life or she was never dead.

Further reading

Studies of Shakespeare and the Renaissance are extensive. Those listed here are chosen as an introduction to a wider field; many include further bibliographies.

Shakespeare's Life

Bryson, Bill. *Shakespeare: The World as Stage*. New York: HarperCollins, 2007.

Honan, Park. *Shakespeare: A Life*. Oxford and New York: Oxford University Press, 1998.

Schoenbaum, Samuel. *William Shakespeare: A Compact Documentary Life*. New York: Oxford University Press, 1977.

Wells, Stanley. *Shakespeare: A Dramatic Life*. London: Sinclair-Stevenson, 1994.

Wood, Michael. *In Search of Shakespeare*. London: BBC, 2003.

The Sonnets and Poems

Dubrow, Heather. *Captive Victors: Shakespeare's Narrative Poems and Sonnets*. Ithaca: Cornell University Press, 1987.

---. "'Incertainties Now Crown Themselves Assur'd': The Politics of Plotting Shakespeare's Sonnets." From *Shakespeare's Sonnets: Critical Essays*. pp.113–62.

Schiffer, James, ed. *Shakespeare's Sonnets: Critical Essays*. New York: Garland, 1999.

Schoenfeldt, Michael, ed. *A Companion to Shakespeare's Sonnets*. Malden, MA: Blackwell, 2007.

Shakespeare, William. *Shakespeare's Sonnets*. Ed. Harold Bloom. New York: Chelsea House, 1987.

---. *The Sonnets and a Lover's Complaint*. Ed. John Kerrigan. Harmondsworth: Penguin, 1986.

Vendler, Helen. *The Art of Shakespeare's Sonnets*. Cambridge, MA: Belknap Press of Harvard University Press, 1997.

Criticism: Shakespeare and Love

Barber, C.L. *Shakespeare's Festive Comedy*. Princeton: Princeton University Press, 1959.

Bloom, Allan. *Shakespeare on Love and Friendship*. Chicago: University of Chicago Press, 2000.

Frye, Northrop. *A Natural Perspective: The Development of Shakespearian Comedy and Romance*. New York: Columbia University Press, 1965.

Line, Jill. *Shakespeare and the Fire of Love*. London: Shepheard-Walwyn, 2004.

Novy, Marianne. *Love's Argument: Gender Relations in Shakespeare*. Chapel Hill, NC: University of North Carolina Press, 1984.

Rose, Mary Beth. *The Expense of Spirit: Love and Sexuality in English Renaissance Drama*. Ithaca: Cornell University Press, 1988.

The Social Context

Bamber, Linda. *Comic Women, Tragic Men: A Study in Gender and Genre in Shakespeare*. Stanford, CA: Stanford University Press, 1982.

Berry, Edward I. *Shakespeare and the Hunt: A Cultural and Social Study*. Cambridge and New York: Cambridge University Press, 2001.

Cook, Ann Jennalie. "Wooing and Wedding: Shakespeare's Dramatic Distortion of the Customs of His Time." From *Shakespeare's Art from a Comparative Aspect*. Ed. Wendell M. Aycock. Lubbock TX: Texas Tech Press, 1981.

Dusinberre, Juliet. *Shakespeare and the Nature of Women*. London: Macmillan, 1975.

Emmison, F.G. *Elizabethan Life: Morals and the Church Courts*. Chelmsford: Essex County Council, 1973.

Hopkins, Lisa. *The Shakespearean Marriage: Merry Wives and Heavy Husbands*. Houndmills, Basingstoke: Macmillan, 1998.

Ingram, Martin. *Church Courts, Sex, and Marriage in England, 1570–1640*. Cambridge: Cambridge University Press, 1987.

Laslett, Peter. *Household and Family in Past Time*. Cambridge: Cambridge University Press, 1972.

---. *Family Life and Illicit Love in Earlier Generations*. Cambridge: Cambridge University Press, 1977.

Rogers, Katherine M. *The Troublesome Helpmate: A History of Misogyny in Literature*. Seattle: University of Washington Press, 1966.

Smith, Bruce R. *Homosexual Desire in Shakespeare's England: A Cultural Poetics.* Chicago: University of Chicago Press, 1991.

Stone, Lawrence. *The Family, Sex and Marriage in England, 1500–1800.* London: Weidenfeld and Nicolson, 1977.

Woodbridge, Linda. *Women and the English Renaissance: Literature and the Nature of Womankind, 1540–1620.* Urbana and Chicago: University of Illinois Press, 1984.

Shakespeare Films

BBC Television/Time-Life have created videos of all the plays. This list includes recent films of particular interest in addition to that series.

Antony and Cleopatra (1985). Director: Jon Scoffield. Principal actors: Janet Suzman, Richard Johnson, Corin Redgrave, Patrick Stewart, Rosemary McHale, Mary Rutherford, Mavis Taylor Blake, Ben Kingsley.

As You Like It (2006). Director: Kenneth Branagh. Principal actors: Bryce Dallas Howard, Kevin Kline, Romola Garai, David Oyelowo, Brian Blessed, Jade Jefferies, Adrian Lester, Janet McTeer, Alfred Molina, Alex Wyndham.

Love's Labour's Lost (2000). Director: Kenneth Branagh. Principal actors: Kenneth Branagh, Richard Clifford, Adrian Lester, Matthew Lillard, Natascha McElhone, Emily Mortimer, Alessandro Nivola, Alicia Silverstone.

The Merchant of Venice (2005). Director: Michael Radford. Principal actors: Al Pacino, Jeremy Irons, Joseph Fiennes, Lynn Collins, Zuleikha Robinson.

A Midsummer Night's Dream (2000). Director: Michael Hoffman. Cast: Rupert Everett, Calista Flockhart, Kevin Kline, Michelle Pfeiffer and Stanley Tucci with Christian Bale, Sophie Marceau and David Strathairn.

Much Ado About Nothing (1993). Directed and adapted by Kenneth Branagh. Principal actors: Kenneth Branagh, Emma Thompson, Michael Keaton, Keanu Reeves, Brian Blessed, Richard Briers, Imelda Staunton, Denzel Washington.

Othello (1995). Director: Oliver Parker. Principal actors: Laurence Fishburne, Irène Jacob, Kenneth Branagh, Nathaniel Parker, Anna Patrick.

Richard III (1995). Director: Richard Loncraine. Principal actors: Ian McKellen, Kristin Scott Thomas, Jim Broadbent, Maggie Smith, Jim Carter, Robert Downey, Jr., Edward Jewesbury, Kate Steavenson-Payne, Dominic West.

Romeo + Juliet (1996). Director: Baz Luhrmann. Principal actors: Leonardo di Caprio, Claire Danes, Brian Dennehy, John Leguizamo, Pete Postlethwaite, Paul Sorvino, Diane Venora.

Romeo and Juliet (1968). Director, Franco Zeffirelli. Principal actors: Olivia Hussey, Leonard Whiting, Milo O'Shea, Michael York, John McEnery, Pat Heywood, Natasha Perry, Robert Stephens.

Shakespeare in Love (1998). Director: John Madden. Principal actors: Gwyneth Paltrow, Joseph Fiennes, Geoffrey Rush, Colin Firth, Ben Affleck, Judi Dench, Tom Wilkinson, Imelda Staunton, Rupert Everett, Simon Callow.

---. Screenplay: Marc Norman and Tom Stoppard. London: Faber and Faber, 1999.

The Taming of the Shrew (1967). Director: Franco Zeffirelli. Principal actors: Richard Burton, Elizabeth Taylor, Michael Hordern, Cyril Cusack, Alfred Lynch, Natasha Pyne, Victor Spinetti, Michael York.

Twelfth Night (1996). Director: Trevor Nunn. Principal actors: Imogen Stubbs, Helena Bonham Carter, Toby Stevens, Ben Kingsley, Nigel Hawthorne, Richard E. Grant, Mel Smith, Imelda Staunton.

Index

Index of First Lines of the Sonnets
(N.b. references are to page numbers, not sonnet numbers)

Acknowledgments

Picture Credits

The publisher would like to thank the following people, museums and photographic libraries for permission to reproduce their material. Every care has been taken to trace copyright holders. However, if we have omitted anyone we apologize and will, if informed, make corrections to any future edition.

Abbreviations: BAL = Bridgeman Art Library, London

Page 2 Attrib. John Taylor: *William Shakespeare*, c.1610 (National Portrait Gallery, London); **7** Hollar: map of London, detail showing the Globe Theatre (Private Collection/JB Archive); **25** Nicholas Hilliard (1547–1619): *Henry Percy, Ninth Earl of Northumberland* (Rijksmuseum, Amsterdam/BAL); **34–35** Ellen Rooney/Robert Harding Travel/Photolibrary.com; **40** Lorenzo Lotto (1480–1556): *Triumph of Chastity*, detail (Private Collection, Rome/Scala, Florence); **46–47** Fotodesign-Hopemann/Photolibrary. com; **49** Tobias Bernhard/zefa/Corbis; **53** Tony Craddock/Getty Images; **56** Dish, probably from Gubbio, 1500–1510 (V&A Museum, London); **59** The Sacred Heart floating in a lake, cut paper work, probably from Austria or southern Germany, c.1800 (Wellcome Library, London); **60** Niccolò Pisano: *An Idyll: Daphnis and Chloe*, detail, c.1500–1501 (The Wallace Collection, London/BAL); **62–63** Marriage gimmel ring, closed and open to show each ring with inscriptions; gold, German, 1575–1600 (V&A Museum, London); **65** Surveyors, printed book, English, c.1590 (The British Library, London/BAL); **72** Gary Cook/Getty Images; **74** Canon in honour of King Henry VIII, celebrating the union of the houses of York and Lancaster, Flanders, c.1516 (The British Library, London. Royal MS 11 E. XI, f.3); **78** Kim Heacox/Getty Images; **83** Three-masted ship; gold, enamelled and pearl pendant, Italian, late 16th century (V&A Museum, London); **85** Giovanni Bellini: *Young Woman at Her Toilet*, detail, 1515 (Kunsthistorisches Museum, Vienna/BAL); **88** The Master of Lyons: Maids and winged hearts c.1500, manuscript detail (Stowe 955 f. 12–13) (British Library, London/BAL); **90** English School: *Charlecote Park*, detail, 18th century (Charlecote Park, Warwickshire/BAL); **93** Maria Mosolova/ Flowerphotos.com; **101** Attrib. John de Critz: *Henry Wriothesley (1573–1624), Third Earl of Southampton*, c.1590–93 (Private Collection/BAL); **105** Lorenzo Lotto: *Signor Marsilio Cassotti and his Wife, Faustina*, 1523 (Prado, Madrid/BAL); **109** Nicholas Hilliard (1547–1619): *A Young Man Leaning Against a Tree Among Roses*, miniature (V&A Museum, London/BAL); **112** Peter Lilja/Getty Images; **123** Eightfish/Getty Images; **127** Parmigianino: *Cupid Carving a Bow*, 1533–4 (Kunsthistorisches Museum, Vienna/BAL); **129** Attrib. John de Critz: *Henry Wriothesley, Third Earl of Southampton*, 1603, detail (Boughton House, Northamptonshire/BAL); **135** Titian: *Venus and Adonis*, 1553, detail (Prado, Madrid/BAL); **141** Mark Bolton/Photolibrary.com; **143** Jan Visscher: *Globe Theatre*, 1616 (British Museum/The Art Archive); **145** Joseph Paton: *The Reconciliation of Oberon and Titania*, 1847, detail (National Gallery of Scotland, Edinburgh/BAL); **151** English School: *Catherine Killigrew, later Lady Jermyn*, c.1595–1600, detail (Ipswich Borough Council Museum and Galleries/BAL); **156** Title page of *Romeo and Juliet*, 1597 (Private Collection/JB Archive); **161** Frank Dicksee: *Romeo and Juliet*, 1884, detail (Southampton City Art Gallery/BAL); **171** Wang Guochen: *Pomegranate Tree*, late 19th century, watercolour on paper (School of Oriental and African Studies Library, University of London/BAL); **175** Robert Glusic/Getty Images; **181** Queen Elizabeth I's Orphorion by John Rose, c.1580 (Helmingham Hall, Suffolk/BAL); **187** Isaac Oliver (c.1565–1617): *Diana*, miniature (V&A Museum/BAL); **191** Attrib. William Larkin: *Anne Cecil, Countess of Stamford*, c.1614, detail (Ranger's House, Blackheath/BAL); **197** English School: *King Richard III*, late 15th century (National Portrait Gallery, London); **205** John Kelly/Getty Images; **211** Sue Kennedy/Flowerphotos.com; **213** Jenny Acheson/Axiom Photographic Agency; **224** Keren Su/Getty Images; **231** IC Productions/Getty Images; **236–237** Sandro Botticelli: *Venus and Mars*, c.1485 (National Gallery, London); **247** Anthony Sandys: *Perdita*, c.1866 (The Maas Gallery, London/ BAL); **253** Dominic Di Saia/Getty Images.

About the Texts

The texts of the plays and poems have been re-edited for this collection. Texts consulted were the collections by David Bevington, Riverside, and Signet, together with the respective Arden editions, and the original quartos and folio versions online at the Internet Shakespeare Editions. I have modernized spelling and punctuation.

Author Acknowledgments

My thanks are due to Roberta Livingstone and Lindsay Gagel, who proofread the introductory materials and annotations, and to Christopher Westhorp, who invited me to take on the rewarding task of distilling years of reading and teaching Shakespeare into this collection. I am especially grateful to the Bevington edition for providing guidance in the matter of annotation.